# The Perfect Pie Book

# The Perfect Pie Book

**Anne Marshall**

OMEGA BOOKS

This edition published 1984 by Omega Books Ltd,
1 West Street, Ware, Hertfordshire, under licence
from the proprietor.

ISBN 1 85007 085 7

Printed and bound in Hong Kong by South China Printing Co.

# CONTENTS

# WEIGHTS AND MEASURES

All the recipes in this book use metric weights and measures in accordance with the Standards Association of Australia.

A reliable set of metric scales, a set of Australian Standard measuring cups (1, ½, ⅓, ¼ cup), a set of Australian Standard measuring spoons (1 tablespoon, 1 teaspoon, ½ teaspoon, ¼ teaspoon), a 1 litre graduated measuring jug and a 250 ml graduated measuring jug are necessary equipment for successful metric cookery. Some, but not all, of this equipment is essential. It is all available at leading kitchenware and hardware shops.

- The Australian Standard measuring cup has a capacity of 250 millilitres (250 ml).
- The Australian Standard tablespoon has a capacity of 20 millilitres (20 ml).
- The Australian Standard teaspoon has a capacity of 5 millilitres (5 ml).

In certain recipes, some imperial weights are given in brackets as a shopping guide, e.g., meat, fish, fruit, vegetables, chocolate, where it is either impossible to buy in metric weights or where it is impractical to measure in a cup.

Temperatures are given in Celsius (°C) with Fahrenheit (°F) temperatures in brackets.

Measurements of length are given in metric with imperial measurements in brackets.

**Important point:** New Zealand, American and Canadian weights and measures are the same except that the Australian Standard measuring tablespoon has a capacity of 20 millilitres (20 ml), whereas the New Zealand, American and Canadian Standard measuring tablespoon has a capacity of 15 millilitres (15 ml).

In Britain, 1 ounce has been rounded down to a metric conversion of 25 grams, whereas in Australia, 1 ounce has been rounded up to a metric conversion of 30 grams. It is therefore important that cooks in Britain follow the metric weights and measures most accurately in this cookbook.

# AMERICAN/BRITISH CONSUMER GUIDE

Even though we all speak the same English language in Australia, America and Britain, the terminology for certain cooking ingredients and methods differs, so I am including this brief guide to help clear up any confusion.

| Australia | America | Britain |
|---|---|---|
| baking powder | baking soda | baking powder |
| cream | light cream | single cream |
| thickened cream | heavy cream | double cream |
| cornflour | cornstarch | cornflour |
| minced beef | ground beef | minced beef |
| pawpaw | papaya | paw paw |
| plain flour | all purpose flour | plain flour |
| prawns | shrimps | prawns |
| king prawns | large shrimps | scampi |
| shallots | green onions/ eschallots | spring onions |
| sour cream | dairy sour cream | soured cream |
| stock cube | bouillon cube | stock cube |
| sugar | sugar | granulated sugar |
| castor sugar | superfine sugar | castor sugar |
| icing sugar | confectioner's sugar | icing sugar |
| tomato paste | tomato paste | tomato purée |
| finely chopped | minced | finely chopped |
| grill | broil | grill |

# INTRODUCTION

The making of pies dates back to Saxon and Norman England, when a flour and water paste was wrapped around a chicken or a piece of ham to keep in the juices during baking. By the Middle Ages, fat was added to the paste, making it more pliable to work with and it also tasted better. Filled pies became popular and elaborately decorated pies were served at court banquets. These were the centre of amusement, for they were often filled with live birds or frogs and even dwarfs. Pies became more and more popular in Victorian England, in particular the pork and game pies, which were packed into the hunt picnic hamper.

Pies reached Australia with the early settlers and the popularity of the meat pie was instant because it required only the basic ingredients, flour, salt, fat, water and a filling of whatever meat was available. Imaginative cooks and chefs have been making pies ever since and today there are endless varieties of both savoury and sweet pies from which to choose. They can be served as party savouries, main courses, picnic food, packed lunches, savoury snacks, suppers, puddings or party desserts. Golden brown, smelling delicious, savoury, juicy or fruity, pies will always be popular in your menu.

*Anne's Perfect Piebook* sets out to help you make an enormous variety of pies. There are meat, chicken, rabbit, fish, vegetable, quiches, pizza, potato-topped and party pies among the savoury ones. There are fruit pies, flans and tarts, custard, meringue, chiffon, crumb crust and cheese-cake pies among the sweet ones. All of these recipes are as easy as pie! This book has been compiled with the assistance of my friends at Thorn Kenwood, the people who make the famous Kenwood Chef kitchen mixer, the ideal companion to any cook really interested in pie-making.

You will see many references to the Kenwood Chef and its K beater in my recipes . Nothing seems to give such good results so quickly.

Happy pie making — and have fun eating them too!

Anne Marshall

# How to cover a pie

Roll pastry to an oval (round for round dish) 4cm (1½ inches) bigger than pie dish and cut a 1cm (½ inch) strip off.

Brush rim of pie dish with cold water, press strip of pastry on, seal at join then brush strip with cold water.

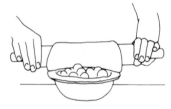

Lift remaining pastry over rolling pin and unroll over top of pie.

Press pastry top onto pastry strip to seal.

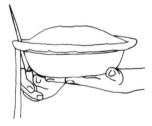

Trim off excess pastry, holding knife at a 15° angle to allow for shrinkage during baking.

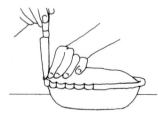

After flaking edges horizontally, flute or scallop with back of knife. Mark 16 scallops for a savoury pie, mark scallops 1cm (½ inch) apart for a sweet pie.

# How to line a flan

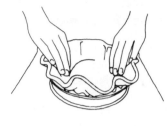

Roll pastry to a round, lift over rolling pin, unroll into flan tin, then press air out from underneath.

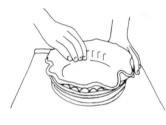

Press pastry over bottom and up sides of tin to prevent shrinkage.

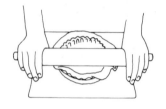

Roll across sharp top of flan tin with rolling pin to trim off extra pastry.

Prick pastry lightly then place a round of greaseproof paper inside pastry case and cover bottom with a layer of baking beans. This is known as baking blind.

# How to make pastry leaves

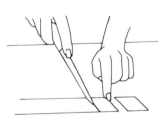

Roll pastry trimmings out thinly, cut a strip 2.5cm (1 inch) wide, then cut across diagonally to make diamond shapes.

Mark veins on leaves with a sharp knife.

# PIE CRUSTS

One of the earliest pie crusts known was a simple flour and water paste called 'huff paste' which was used to wrap around ham and poultry to keep the juices in during baking. Eventually fat was added to this paste to make it more pliable. Many years later, the French developed flaky pastry, possibly by accident.

Today we have pie crusts galore. Some are short and crisp as in short crust and rich short crust pastry, or richer as in the French pâte brisée and pâte sucrée, others are light and flaky as in puff, rough puff and flaky pastries. Then there is choux, named after the French for cabbage because it puffs out like one when baked. There is also the English gentleman's flavoursome favourite, hot water crust pastry which is used to envelope pork pies. Healthy pastries too, like wholemeal wheatgerm pastries and low cholesterol pastry, are here, and nutritious also means delicious. For a quick crust, use a crumb crust or for something traditional use a pizza or scone dough. Then there are some surprises like sour cream, cheese, lard and American pastries.

Detailed instructions are given in this chapter for making all these pastries with your Kenwood mixer and they may also be mixed in a food processor.

## Tips

Keep everything cool for pastry making. The ideal is a stainless steel bowl like the Kenwood bowl for mixing in and a marble slab for rolling out on.

Keep your hands cool when handling pastry—this can be done by holding them under cold running water for a few minutes.

Always roll pastry out on a *lightly* floured surface, otherwise you add more flour to the basic proportions.

Roll pastry forwards and backwards with short, sharp rolls—never roll sideways as it gives an uneven thickness.

Wrap pastry securely in greaseproof paper before chilling in refrigerator; clear plastic wrap tends to make it sweat.

Do not turn pastry over during rolling.

# Short Crust Pastry

*Makes 250 g (8 oz) pastry, sufficient to cover and decorate a 1 litre (4 cup) oval pie dish, or to line or cover and decorate a 23 cm (9 inch) pie plate.*

**250 g (2 cups) plain flour**
**pinch of salt**
**60 g (2 tablespoons) butter or firm margarine**
**60 g (2 tablespoons) lard**
**4 tablespoons cold water**

Sift flour and salt into the Kenwood bowl, then add butter and lard cut into small cubes. Using the K beater, turn mixer on at minimum speed and increase gradually to speed 2 as the fats break up, then continue mixing at speed 2 until mixture resembles fine breadcrumbs, approx. 2½ minutes. Add cold water and mix at speed 2 until mixture forms a dough which leaves the sides of the bowl clean; switch off immediately. Turn dough onto a lightly floured board or marble slab and knead very lightly with clean cool hands, then wrap in greaseproof paper and chill in refrigerator for at least 30 minutes before use.

**Note:** This pastry dough freezes well. It may also be stored for a few days in a plastic bag in the refrigerator.

# Sweet Short Crust Pastry

*Makes 185 g (6 oz) pastry, sufficient to cover a 1 litre (4 cup) oval pie dish or a 23 cm (9 inch) pie plate or to line a shallow 20 or 23 cm (8 or 9 inch) flan tin.*

**185 g (1½ cups) plain flour**
**pinch of salt**
**2 teaspoons castor sugar**
**90 g (3 tablespoons) unsalted butter**
**2-3 tablespoons cold water**

Make pastry as for Short Crust Pastry, adding the sugar to the flour and salt in the Kenwood bowl. Chill well before use.

**Note:** As for Short Crust Pastry.

# Rich Short Crust Pastry

*Makes 250 g (8 oz) pastry, sufficient to cover and decorate, or to line a 23 cm (9 inch) pie plate; 185 g (¾ quantity) is sufficient to line a 20 or 23 cm (8 or 9 inch) flan tin.*

**250 g (2 cups) plain flour**
**125 g (½ cup) butter**
**1 tablespoon castor sugar**
**pinch of salt**
**1 egg yolk**
**2 teaspoons lemon juice**
**1-2 tablespoons cold water**

Sift flour onto a square of greaseproof paper. Place butter, sugar and salt in the Kenwood bowl, switch to minimum speed, tip in flour and gradually increase speed to 2 as the butter mixture breaks up. Mix until mixture resembles fine breadcrumbs, approx. 1½ minutes. Stir the egg yolk, lemon juice and water together, add to mixture and mix at speed 1 for approx. 30-45 seconds. Switch off as soon as ingredients are incorporated. Knead dough lightly on a lightly floured board or marble slab, then wrap in greaseproof paper and allow to rest for 30 minutes in the refrigerator before use.

**Note:** As for Short Crust Pastry.

# One-Stage Short Crust Pastry

*Makes 185 g (6 oz) pastry, sufficient to cover a 1 litre (4 cup) oval pie dish or a 23 cm (9 inch) round pie plate or to line a shallow 23 cm (9 inch) flan tin or a deep 20 cm (8 inch) flan tin.*

**125 g (½ cup) soft margarine**
**1 tablespoon cold water**
**185 g (1½ cups) plain flour, sifted**

Place soft margarine, water and 2 tablespoons of the measured flour into the Kenwood bowl. Using the K beater, turn mixer on at minimum speed and mix for 15 seconds, add remaining flour and increase gradually to speed 2 for 1 minute or until mixture forms a firm dough which leaves sides of bowl clean. Turn dough onto a lightly floured board and knead lightly until smooth, then wrap in greaseproof paper and chill in refrigerator for at least 30 minutes before use.

**Note:** This pastry freezes well. It may also be stored for a few days in a plastic bag in the refrigerator.

# Low Cholesterol Short Crust Pastry

*Makes 185 g (6 oz) pastry, sufficient to cover a 1 litre (4 cup) oval pie dish or a 23 cm (9 inch) pie plate or to line a 20 or 23 cm (8 or 9 inch) flan tin.*

**125 g (½ cup) polyunsaturated margarine**
**1 tablespoon cold water**
**185 g (1½ cups) plain flour, sifted**

Make pastry as for One-Stage Short Crust Pastry. Wrap in greaseproof paper and chill in refrigerator for at least 30 minutes before use.

**Note:** Freezes well, may also be stored in a plastic bag in refrigerator for a few days.

# Pâte Brisée

*Makes 185 g (6oz) pastry, sufficient to line a deep 20 cm or shallow 23 cm (8 or 9 inch) flan tin.*

**125 g (½ cup) chilled butter**
**185 g (1½ cups) plain flour**
**¼ teaspoon salt**
**3-5 tablespoons iced water**

Cut butter into cubes and place in the Kenwood bowl. Sift flour and salt together onto a square of greaseproof paper. Add a little flour to the butter and mix with K beater at minimum speed until mixture begins to break up, then gradually add remaining flour and increase speed to 2 and mix for 2 minutes. Increase speed to 3 for ½-1 minute more, or until mixture resembles fine breadcrumbs. Add 3 tablespoons iced water all at once, and mix at speed 3 for 10 seconds. If dough has not come together, add remaining water gradually on minimum speed until mixture leaves side of bowl clean. Knead pastry lightly on a lightly floured marble slab or board until smooth, then wrap in greaseproof paper and chill in refrigerator for ½-1 hour or until firm.

**Note:** Freezes well and stores well in a plastic bag in refrigerator for a few days.

# Pâte Sucrée

*Makes 250 g (8 oz) pastry, sufficient to line a deep 20 cm (8 inch) or a shallow 23 cm (9 inch) flan tin.*

**125 g (½ cup) butter, chilled**
**250 g (2 cups) plain flour**
**60 g (½ cup) pure icing sugar**
**2 egg yolks or 1 egg**
**1 teaspoon water (only if necessary)**

Cut butter into cubes and place in the Kenwood bowl. Sift flour and icing sugar together onto a square of greaseproof paper. Add a little flour to butter and mix with K beater at minimum speed until butter begins to break up, then gradually add remaining flour, and increase speed to 2 for 2 minutes, then increase speed to 3 for a further 30 seconds, or until mixture resembles fine breadcrumbs. Reduce speed to 1, add egg and mix until dough comes together. If dough is too dry and will not come together, add water and mix to bind. Knead dough lightly on a lightly floured marble slab or board just until smooth, then wrap in greaseproof paper and chill in refrigerator for ½-1 hour or until firm.

**Note:** As for Pâte Brisée.

# Cheese Pastry

*Makes 185 g (6 oz) pastry, sufficient for 24 Smoked Fish Pyramids.*

**125 g (1 cup) Cheddar cheese, grated**
**2 tablespoons finely grated Parmesan**
   **cheese**
**125 g (½ cup) butter**
**185 g (1½ cups) plain flour**
**pinch each of salt, white pepper and**
   **cayenne pepper**
**2 egg yolks**

Grate cheese in a food processor. Place cheeses and butter in the Kenwood bowl and mix at speed 2 until creamy. Sift flour and seasoning onto a square of grease-proof paper. Add sieved flour and egg yolks to bowl and mix at speed 2 until mixture forms a stiff dough, about 2 minutes. Knead dough lightly on a lightly floured pastry board until smooth, then wrap in greaseproof paper and chill for 30 minutes before use.

# Sour Cream Pastry

*Makes 185 g (6 oz) pastry, sufficient to cover a 1 litre (4 cup) oval pie dish or a 23 cm (9 inch) pie plate.*

**185 g (1½ cups) plain flour**
**90 g (3 tablespoons) butter, chilled**
**125 ml (½ cup) sour cream**

Sift flour into bowl. Cut butter into small cubes and add to flour. Beat with K beater at speed 2 for 1 minute 30 seconds. Increase speed to 4 for a further 15 seconds or until mixture resembles coarse breadcrumbs. Add sour cream and beat at speed 1 for 25 seconds, or until pastry leaves sides of bowl clean. Knead dough very lightly on a lightly floured board into a smooth, round shape. Wrap in greaseproof paper and chill for at least 30 minutes before use.

# Wholemeal Pastry

*Makes 250 g (8 oz) pastry, sufficient to line and cover four round 8 cm (3 inch) pie tins, or to line a shallow 23 cm (9 inch) flan tin.*

**250 g (2 cups) wholemeal flour, medium or**
   **course ground**
**1 teaspoon salt**
**125 g (½ cup) butter or firm margarine**
**cold water to mix**

Place wholemeal flour and salt in the Kenwood bowl, add butter and continue as for Short Crust Pastry (page 11).

**Note:** Stores well in a plastic bag in refrigerator for a few days, also freezes well.

# Wholemeal Wheatgerm Pastry

*Makes 185 g (6 oz) pastry, sufficient to line or cover a round 23 cm (9 inch) pie plate, or to cover a 1 litre (4 cup) oval pie dish or to line a shallow 23 cm (9 inch) flan tin.*

**125 g (1 cup) wholemeal flour**
**60 g (1 cup) wheatgerm**
**90 g (3 tablespoons) polyunsaturated margarine**
**3 tablespoons iced water**

Mix flour and wheatgerm together in the Kenwood bowl. Add margarine and mix at speed 2 for about 60 seconds or until mixture resembles fine breadcrumbs. Add water, a tablespoon at a time, still mixing at speed 2 for approx. 45-60 seconds or until mixture leaves side of bowl clean, and forms a ball around the K beater. Knead pastry on a lightly floured board until smooth, then shape into a round. Wrap in greaseproof paper and chill in refrigerator for at least 30 minutes.

**Note:** This pastry dough freezes well. It may also be stored for a few days in a plastic bag in the refrigerator. This is a low cholesterol pastry.

# Low Cholesterol Wholemeal Pastry

*Makes 250 g (8 oz) wholemeal pastry, sufficient to line or cover a round 23 cm (9 inch) pie plate.*

**125 g (½ cup) polyunsaturated margarine**
**2 tablespoons cold water**
**250 g (2 cups) wholemeal flour**

Make as for One-Stage Pastry (page 12).

**Note:** Freezes well, may also be stored for a few days in a plastic bag in the refrigerator.

# American Pastry

*Makes 250 g (8 oz) pastry, sufficient for lining, covering and decorating a 23 cm (9 inch) pie plate or for covering 2 x 1 litre (4 cup) oval pie dishes.*

**155 g (½ cup + 1 tablespoon) lard**
**3 tablespoons water**
**250 g (2 cups) self-raising flour**

Place lard and water in the Kenwood bowl and mix with the K beater at speed 2 until soft and creamy. Add sifted flour, then mix at minimum speed, gradually increasing to speed 2 until mixture resembles breadcrumbs, about 1½-2 minutes. Knead dough lightly, then wrap securely in greaseproof paper and chill in refrigerator for at least 30 minutes.

# Lard Pastry

*Makes 155 g (5 oz) dough, sufficient to line a 23 cm (9 inch) pie plate, or flan tin.*

**155 g (1¼ cups) plain flour**
**1 teaspoon sugar**
**pinch of salt**
**60 g (¼ cup) lard**
**75 g (approx. ⅓ cup) butter**
**2-3 tablespoons iced water**

Sift dry ingredients into the Kenwood bowl. Cut lard and butter into small pieces and add to dry ingredients. Mix ingredients at speed 1, increasing to 2 for 30 seconds, then increase to speed 3 for a further 30 seconds or until mixture is combined but resembles coarse crumbs. Add water a tablespoon at a time, mixing at speed 3, and mix until mixture comes together to form a dough, approx. 15 seconds. Knead dough gently on a lightly floured board until smooth. Wrap in greaseproof paper and chill in refrigerator for 30 minutes or until required.

# Hot Water Crust Pastry

*Makes 375 g (12 oz) pastry, sufficient to make either 1 x 12 cm (5 inch) pork pie, or four individual 8 cm (3 inch) pork pies, or to line a 20 cm (8 inch) game pie mould.*

**375 g (3 cups) plain flour**
**1 teaspoon salt**
**125 g (½ cup) lard**
**250 ml (1 cup) water**
**1 egg yolk**

Sift flour and salt into the warm Kenwood bowl. Heat lard and water together in a saucepan, then bring rapidly to the boil. Quickly pour boiling lard and water mixture onto flour, and using the K beater, mix at minimum speed for 15 seconds. Add egg yolk and continue to beat for a further 15 seconds. Increase to speed 2 and beat for a further 30 seconds or until mixture leaves side of bowl clean and forms a smooth ball around the K beater. Wrap in greaseproof paper and allow to rest at room temperature for 20-30 minutes before use.

**Note:** This pastry must be kept warm at all times, not cold.

# Puff Pastry

*Makes 500 g (1 lb) pastry, sufficient to cover 2 x 1 litre (4 cup) oval pie dishes or 2 x 23 cm (9 inch) pie plates.*

**500 g (2 cups) butter or margarine, unsalted if possible**
**500 g (4 cups) plain flour**
**1 teaspoon lemon juice**
**cold water to mix**

Shape butter into a flat square pat and place in refrigerator until cool and firm. Sieve flour into the Kenwood bowl and using the K beater mix in lemon juice and sufficient cold water, on minimum speed, to form an elastic dough. Turn onto a floured pastry board or marble slab and knead lightly until paste is smooth and elastic and not sticky. Roll out on a lightly floured surface to a rectangle twice as big as the butter pat. Place butter on top half of dough, fold bottom half over and roll out evenly to a long strip, taking care butter does not break through. Fold strip of pastry in three and cool in refrigerator for 10-15 minutes. Place pastry on rolling surface with folded edge to the right, roll and fold twice, placing folded edge alternately to the left, then return to the refrigerator to cool. Repeat rolling and folding processes until pastry has had seven rolls and folds, chilling whenever necessary. Wrap dough in greaseproof paper and chill well before use.

**Note:** This pastry freezes well.

# Rough Puff Pastry

*Makes 250 g (8 oz) pastry, sufficient to line and cover a 23 cm (9 inch) round pie plate or to cover and decorate a 1 litre (4 cup) oval pie dish with a little left over for some pasties or turnovers.*

**250 g (2 cups) plain flour**
**pinch of salt**

**90 g (3 tablespoons) butter or firm margarine**
**90 g (3 tablespoons) lard**
**3 tablespoons cold water**

Sift flour and salt into the Kenwood bowl. Mix butter and lard together on an enamel plate with a round-bladed knife until well blended, then chill until firm. Cut fat into even-sized pieces the size of a walnut and drop into flour, tossing each piece well to coat it. Add cold water and, using the K beater, mix at minimum speed for 15 seconds. Turn dough on to a lightly floured board and roll out to an oblong, approx. 15 x 25 cm (6 x 10 inches). Fold in three and make a half turn so that an open end faces you. Repeat rolling, folding and turning twice more. Refrigerate dough at any stage when it becomes too soft and greasy to handle. Wrap in greaseproof paper and refrigerate for at least 30 minutes before use.

**Note:** Stores well for a few days in a plastic bag in the refrigerator. This pastry dough also freezes well.

# Choux Pastry

*Makes 60 g (2 oz) pastry.*

**125 ml (½ cup) water**
**60 g (2 tablespoons) butter**
**60 g (½ cup) plain flour**
**¼ teaspoon salt**
**2 eggs**
**few drops vanilla essence**

Place water and butter in a saucepan and bring to boiling point over a medium heat. Remove immediately from heat to prevent evaporation. Quickly stir in sifted flour and salt all at once, using a wooden spoon. Return saucepan to a low heat and beat mixture 1-2 minutes, or until mixture forms a smooth paste which leaves the side of pan clean. Remove from heat and place in the Kenwood bowl. Beat eggs and, using the K beater at speed 2, beat them into the mixture in four stages, beating well after each addition until no trace of egg remains. Finally beat in vanilla essence.

# Savoury Choux Pastry

*Makes 125 g (4 oz) pastry.*

**250 ml (1 cup) water**
**90 g (3 tablespoons) butter**
**125 g (1 cup) plain flour**
**pinch of salt**
**3 eggs**
**3 tablespoons grated Parmesan cheese**
**salt and pepper**
**mustard powder**

Prepare as for Choux Pastry (page 15) but beat eggs and beat into the mixture using K beater at speed 2 in 6 stages, beating well after each addition, until no trace of egg remains and mixture is smooth and shiny. Finally beat in Parmesan cheese and season to taste with salt, pepper and mustard powder.

# Flaky Pastry

*Makes 250 g (8 oz) pastry, sufficient to cover and decorate a 1 litre (4 cup) oval pie dish or cover a 23 cm (9 inch) pie plate.*

**250 g (2 cups) plain flour**
**pinch of salt**
**90 g (3 tablespoons) butter or firm margarine**
**90 g (3 tablespoons) lard**
**125 ml (½ cup) cold water**

Sift flour and salt into the Kenwood bowl. Mix fats together on an enamel plate with a round-bladed knife and shape into a square block. Add a quarter of the mixed fat to the flour, mix at minimum speed, then increase to speed 2 and mix until mixture resembles fine breadcrumbs, about 2 minutes. Stop mixer, then add water and mix at speed 2 to a firm dough which leaves side of bowl cleanly, adding more water if necessary. Knead the dough lightly on a lightly floured board until smooth, then roll out to an oblong approx. 15 x 25 cm (6 x 10 inches). Put another quarter of the mixed fat in flakes or small pieces on the top two-thirds of the dough. Fold in three, folding the bottom third up and the top third down. This gives you even layers of dough and fat. Half turn the pastry, so that an open end faces you, and roll out again to an oblong. Repeat flaking, folding and rolling of dough twice more. Refrigerate the dough at any stage when it becomes too soft and greasy to handle. Fold pastry into three once more, wrap in greaseproof paper and refrigerate until required.

**Note:** This pastry will keep well for a few days in the refrigerator in a plastic bag. It also freezes well.

# Piragi Dough

*Makes 250 g (8 oz) dough.*

**125 ml (½ cup) lukewarm milk**
**15 g (½ oz) compressed yeast or 1 x 7 g packet (1¾ teaspoons) dry yeast**
**½ teaspoon sugar**
**250 g (2 cups) plain flour**
**1 egg, lightly beaten**
**2 tablespoons butter, melted and cooled**
**1 teaspoon salt**

Firstly, warm the Kenwood bowl by filling with hot water, then dry thoroughly. Pour lukewarm milk into the bowl, sprinkle with yeast and sugar and stir to dissolve. Cover bowl with a clean tea towel and leave to stand in a warm place for 10 minutes. Mix in 1 cup flour, cover again and leave to rise for 40 minutes, or until double in bulk. Stir in remaining flour, egg, butter and salt, then beat with a dough hook at speed 3 for 20-30 seconds or until smooth. Cover dough with a tea towel and allow to stand in a warm place for 1 hour or until double in bulk. Punch dough down by hand until smooth or knead at speed 3 using the dough hook for 15 seconds. Use dough as required.

# Pizza Dough

*Makes 400 g (approx. 13 oz) dough, sufficient for 2 pizzas.*

**250 ml (1 cup) lukewarm water**
**30 g (1 oz) compressed yeast or 2 x 7 g packets (3½ teaspoons) dry yeast**
**3 tablespoons olive oil**
**400 g (3 cups + 2 tablespoons) plain flour**
**1½ teaspoons salt**
**¼ teaspoon white pepper**

Place lukewarm water in the warmed Kenwood bowl. Crumble yeast into water and stir until smooth, then stir in olive oil. Sift flour, salt and pepper over yeast mixture and mix in thoroughly with a wooden spoon. Using a dough hook, beat the dough at speed 3 for 1 minute. Place dough in a clean, warm, greased mixing bowl and turn dough over to grease it all over. Cover with a clean tea towel and leave in a warm place for 1-1½ hours or until double in bulk. Turn risen dough out onto a lightly floured board and knead five to six times by hand. It will collapse very quickly at this stage. Use dough as required.

**Note:** Freezes well.

# Scone Dough

*Makes 250 g (8 oz) dough, sufficient for 1 pizza.*

**60 g (2 tablespoons) soft butter or
 polyunsaturated margarine
250 g (2 cups) self-raising flour
1 teaspoon salt
4 tablespoons milk
1 egg**

Place all ingredients in given order in the Kenwood bowl and mix with the K beater for 30 seconds, increasing speed to 3. Turn dough out onto a lightly floured board and toss lightly until smooth. Use dough as required.

# Crumb Crust

*Makes 1 crumb crust.*

**225 g packet wholemeal or plain sweet
 biscuits
125 g (½ cup) butter**

Break biscuits in half and in a blender, about a third at a time, mix at maximum speed for 20 seconds or until biscuits are crushed. This can also be done in a food processor. Pour biscuit crumbs into the Kenwood bowl. Melt butter in a saucepan over a low heat, add to biscuit crumbs and mix thoroughly. Cool slightly, then press into a 20 or 23 cm (8 or 9 inch) pie plate, flan ring or spring form tin. Refrigerate until firm, about 1 hour.

**Note:** Less butter may be needed if the biscuits are rich.

# MEAT PIES

Thankfully, there are far more varieties of meat pie than the infamous Australian meat pie that we all joke about. Pies arrived in this country with the first settlers and Steak and Kidney Pie, Beef and Burgundy Pie, Veal and Ham Pie and Cornish Pasties are still often served in many a home over this continent.
Meat pies are rich with juices and hearty meaty fillings, and need to be complemented with a crisp, short-textured or light, flaky crust. Traditionally the crust of a meat pie is decorated with leaves and flowers moulded out of the pastry trimmings, and it is glazed with beaten egg. The edges are flaked and fluted with sixteen scallops. In this way you can distinguish a savoury meat pie from a fruit pie. Detailed instructions for covering and decorating a meat pie traditionally are given in the recipe for Steak and Kidney Pie.

# Tips

Use a china pie holder or an upturned egg cup in the centre of a meat pie to hold the centre of the pastry up.

Always place your pies on a baking tray as it catches the juices if it boils over and it also makes it easier to turn the pie around and remove it from the oven.

# Empanadas

*Makes 12.*

**250 g (1 quantity) short crust pastry (see page 11)**

**Filling:**
**1 onion, finely chopped**
**1 tablespoon olive oil**
**125 ml (½ cup) water**
**250 g (8 oz) topside beef**
**1 tablespoon seedless raisins**
**1 teaspoon chilli powder**
**½ teaspoon paprika pepper**
**¼ teaspoon ground cumin**
**½ teaspoon salt**
**freshly ground black pepper**
**2 hard-boiled eggs**
**12 green olives, stoned**

Prepare pastry according to recipe and chill well.

*Filling:* Chop onion in either a blender or a food processor. Place onion, olive oil and water in a small frying pan, bring to the boil over a high heat and boil continuously until water has evaporated. Trim beef and mince in either a Kenwood mincer attachment or a food processor. Add minced beef to frying pan and stir over heat until browned on all sides. Remove from heat. Cover raisins with boiling water, stand for 10 minutes, then drain well. Stir raisins, chilli powder, paprika, cumin, salt and pepper into beef mixture and leave to cool. Shell hard-boiled eggs and cut each into eight wedges lengthways.

*To finish empanadas:* Roll pastry dough out thinly on a lightly floured board and cut out twelve 12 cm (5 inch) rounds. Place 1½ tablespoons filling in the centre of each round. Place a wedge of egg and a stoned olive on top of meat filling. Brush edge of pastry rounds with cold water and fold in half to form a crescent, pressing edges together firmly to seal. Roll edges over at an angle of 45 degrees to create a rope effect. Place empanadas on a baking tray and bake towards the top of a hot oven at 200°C (400°F) for 15-20 minutes until crisp and golden. Cool on a wire cooling tray. Serve warm for a snack meal or cold for a picnic or packed lunch.

English Pork Pie and Pork and Apple Pies
*(see page 24)*

# Cornish Pasties

*Makes 6.*

**250 g (1 quantity) short crust pastry (see page 11)**

*Filling:*
**250 g (8 oz) topside beef**
**1 small onion, chopped**
**2 small potatoes, chopped**
**½ cup chopped turnip**
**¾ teaspoon salt**
**½ teaspoon white pepper**
**beaten egg to glaze**

Prepare pastry according to recipe and chill well.

*Filling:* Trim beef and cut into 5 cm (2 inch) pieces. Mix beef to 5 mm (¼ inch) pieces in a food processor. Chop onion, potato and turnip in either a blender or a food processor. Mix meat, onion, potato and turnip with salt and pepper in a mixing bowl.

*To finish pasties:* Roll pastry dough out thinly on a lightly floured board to a large circle. Cut pastry into 15 cm (6 inch) rounds, using an upturned saucer and a sharp knife or pastry wheel. Gather scraps of dough together, roll out again and cut out rounds until there are six altogether. Turn rounds of pastry over so that rolled side is underneath. Divide filling between the six rounds. Brush edges of pastry with cold water and fold the pastry rounds in half, upwards, enclosing the filling, and press edges together well to seal. To finish edges correctly in the true Cornish style, roll them over tightly, starting at one end and finishing at the other. Alternatively, flute the sealed edge between the finger and thumb. Place pasties on a greased baking tray and brush with beaten egg. Bake in the centre of a hot oven at 220°C (425°F) for 15 minutes, then reduce temperature to moderately slow, 160°C (325°F) and continue baking for a further 30 minutes or until the pasties are golden brown and filling is cooked. Cool on a wire cooling tray for a few minutes, then serve hot for lunch or for a snack.

# Barbecued Lamb Pie

*Serves 6.*

**250 g (1 quantity) short crust pastry (see page 11)**

*Filling:*
**1 kg (2 lb) lean boneless leg of lamb**
**1 tablespoon brown sugar**
**2 tablespoons dry sherry**
**4 tablespoons Worcestershire sauce**
**30 g (1 tablespoon) butter or margarine**
**3 tablespoons tomato sauce**
**3 tablespoons fruit sauce or chutney**
**½ teaspoon vinegar**
**¼ teaspoon Tabasco sauce**
**beaten egg to glaze**

Prepare pastry according to recipe and chill well.

*Filling:* Trim fat and tissues from lamb and cut lamb into 2.5 cm (1 inch) cubes. Place lamb, sugar, sherry and Worcestershire sauce in a casserole. Cover and cook in a moderate oven at 180°C (350°F) for 1 hour or until tender. Transfer lamb with a slotted spoon to a pie dish. Spoon 4 tablespoons of the lamb juice over. Heat remaining ingredients together, except egg glaze, until combined, then pour over the lamb and leave to cool.

*To finish pie:* Roll pastry out to an oval and cover pie as for Steak and Kidney Pie (see page 22). Brush pastry with beaten egg, place pie on a baking tray and bake towards the top of a hot oven at 200°C (400°F) for 25-30 minutes. Serve hot with creamed potatoes and buttered cabbage.

Homestead Chicken Pie
*(see page 29)*

# Steak and Kidney Pie

*Serves 4-6.*

**250 g (1 quantity) short crust pastry
(see page 11)**

*Filling:*
**750 g (1½ lb) stewing steak, chuck, skirt
  or blade
250 g (8 oz) ox kidney
2 tablespoons plain flour
2 teaspoons salt
½ teaspoon pepper
1 onion or 8 shallots, chopped
125 ml (½ cup) water or red wine
beaten egg to glaze**

Prepare pastry according to recipe and
chill well.

*Filling:* Trim fat and gristle off meat and
cut meat into cubes. Wash kidney in cold,
salted water, dry, remove skin and tubes
with kitchen scissors, and cut kidney into
very small cubes. Toss steak and kidney in
flour, salt and pepper. Place steak and
kidney in a casserole. Chop onion in a
blender or food processor, add to casserole with water and cook in a slow oven
at 150°C (300°F) for 2 hours. Remove from
oven and leave until cold.
Alternatively, cut trimmed meat into 8 x 4
cm (3 x 1½ inch) strips and beat with a
meat mallet or rolling pin to tenderize. Prepare kidney as above in small cubes. Place
a cube of kidney on each strip of beef, roll
up tightly and roll in flour mixed with salt
and pepper. Place in a small casserole, so
that rolls cover the bottom neatly without
unrolling, add onion and water and cook in
oven as above. This is a more traditional
method of preparation.

*To finish pie:* Place steak and kidney filling
in a 1 litre (4 cup) oval pie dish. Place a pie
funnel or upturned egg cup in centre to
hold up the pastry, and leave filling to cool.
Roll pastry out to an oval, 4 cm (1½
inches) wider all round than the pie dish.
Cut off a 1 cm (½ inch) strip from round
edge of pastry. Brush rim of pie dish with
cold water and press strip of pastry onto it,
sealing neatly. Brush pastry strip with more
cold water. Lift remaining oval of pastry
over a rolling pin and unroll over pie dish.
Press gently to seal edges. Trim, then flake
edges and mark with sixteen scallops.
Make two slits at each end of pie with a
skewer or sharp knife to allow steam to
escape. Decorate centre of pie with a rose

and leaves cut out of pastry trimmings.
Brush pastry with lightly beaten egg.
Stand pie dish on a baking tray and bake
in a hot oven at 220°C (425°F) for 30
minutes or until pastry is golden brown and
cooked. Serve hot with creamed potatoes,
buttered carrots and sprouts.

# Beef and Burgundy Pies

*Serves 6.*

**500 g (double quantity) puff, rough puff or
  flaky pastry (see pages 15, 16)**

*Filling:*
**1 kg (2 lb) topside beef or chuck steak
250 g (8 oz) ox or lamb kidney
6 tablespoons plain flour
2 teaspoons salt
½ teaspoon pepper
90 g (3 tablespoons) butter or margarine
3 tablespoons oil
1 large onion, chopped
2 cloves garlic, crushed
185 g (6 oz) mushrooms, sliced
300 ml (approx. 1¼ cups) burgundy
beaten egg to glaze**

Prepare pastry according to recipe and
chill well.

*Filling:* Trim fat and tissues from beef and
cut meat into 2.5 cm (1 inch) cubes. Skin
and trim kidney and cut into 1 cm (½ inch)
cubes. Mix flour, salt and pepper together,
and toss beef and kidney in seasoned flour
until coated. Heat 2 tablespoons butter and
the oil in a heavy frying pan and fry the
beef and kidney quickly, with any extra
seasoned flour, until browned. Place beef
and kidney in a casserole. Add remaining
butter to pan and gently fry onion
(chopped in a food processor) and garlic
for 3 minutes, stirring occasionally. Add
sliced mushrooms (also prepared in food
processor) to pan and fry for 2 minutes.
Add burgundy to pan and bring to the boil,
stirring to dissolve pan sediments. Pour
over the beef and kidney. Cover casserole
and cook in a moderate oven at 180°C
(350°F) for 30 minutes, then reduce to
160°C (325°F) for ½-1 hour or until beef is
tender.

*To finish pies:* Divide beef mixture between
six individual 250 ml (1 cup) oval pie dishes
or ovenproof dishes and allow to cool. Roll
pastry out thinly and cut out six tops for

the pie dishes. Brush rim of each pie dish with cold water, place pastry over filling and press onto rim to seal firmly. Flake and flute edges. Decorate pies with leaves cut out of pastry trimmings. Brush tops of pies with beaten egg, then make a slit in the top of each one. Stand pie dishes on a baking tray and bake towards the top of a very hot oven at 230°C (450°F) for 15 minutes or until puffed and golden brown. Serve pies hot, topped with a sprig of parsley accompanied by a green vegetable.

# Veal and Ham Pie

*Serves 4.*

**250 g (1 quantity) puff, rough puff or flaky pastry (see pages 15, 16)**

*Filling:*
**500 g (1 lb) lean pie veal**
**1 onion, quartered**
**1 bouquet garni**
**250 ml (1 cup) water**
**30 g (1 tablespoon) butter or margarine**
**30 g (2 tablespoons) plain flour**
**125 ml (½ cup) milk**
**125 g (4 oz) button mushrooms**
**1 teaspoon salt**
**¼ teaspoon pepper**
**pinch of dried thyme**
**125 g (4 oz) cooked ham, in a piece**
**beaten egg to glaze**

Prepare pastry according to recipe and chill well.

*Filling:* Cut veal into cubes. Place veal, onion, bouquet garni and water into a heavy pan, cover and simmer for 30 minutes or cook in a pressure cooker for 10 minutes. Measure and reserve ½ cup stock. Melt butter, stir in flour and stir over a medium heat for 1 minute. Add reserved stock and milk and bring to the boil, stirring continuously. Add mushrooms, salt, pepper and thyme and simmer for 1 minute. Remove from heat and stir in the veal. Cut ham into cubes and stir into mixture. Adjust seasoning to taste.

*To finish pie:* Pour filling into an oval pie dish with a pie funnel or an upturned egg cup in the centre. Roll out pastry to an oval shape 4 cm (1½ inches) wider all round than the pie dish. Cut a strip 1 cm (½ inch) wide from around edge of pastry. Brush rim of pie dish with cold water, place

pastry rim on this and press firmly to seal. Brush pastry strip with more cold water. Lift remaining oval of pastry onto a rolling pin and unroll over pie dish. Seal, trim, flake and flute edges. Decorate pie with pastry leaves made from pastry trimmings. Brush top of pie (not flaked edges) with beaten egg, place pie dish on a baking tray and bake in a hot oven at 220°C (425°F) for 35-40 minutes or until pastry is golden brown and puffed. Serve hot with creamed potatoes and green peas.

# Scottish Mince Pie

*Serves 6-8.*

**375 g (1½ quantities) flaky or rough puff pastry (see pages 15, 16)**

*Filling:*
**30 g (1 tablespoon) dripping or oil**
**1 onion, finely chopped**
**2 stalks celery, finely chopped**
**500 g (1 lb) finely minced beef**
**1 teaspoon salt**
**¼ teaspoon pepper**
**2 tablespoons tomato paste**
**2 tablespoons water**
**1 tablespoon oatmeal**
**beaten egg for glazing**

Prepare pastry according to recipe and chill well.

*Filling:* Heat dripping in a heavy pan and fry onion and celery (chopped in a food processor or blender) for 5 minutes. Add beef (minced in a food processor or Kenwood mincer attachment) and fry, stirring occasionally, until meat is browned. Stir in salt, pepper, tomato paste, water and oatmeal and bring to the boil. Remove from heat and cool.

*To finish pie:* Roll out half pastry to a round shape and line a 23 cm (9 inch) round pie dish. Place mince mixture into pastry shell. Roll out remaining pastry to a round and cover the pie. Seal, trim and decorate edge of pie. Decorate pie with a rose and leaves made from extra pastry. Glaze with beaten egg. Place pie on a baking tray and bake in a hot oven at 220°C (425°F) for 20-30 minutes, or until pastry is cooked and golden brown. Serve hot with creamed potatoes and buttered celery or sprouts.

# English Pork Pie

*Serves 4-6.*

**375 g (1 quantity) hot water crust pastry
(see page 14)**

*Filling:*
**1 kg (2 lb) lean boneless pork
3 tablespoons stock or water
¼ teaspoon dried sage leaves
1 teaspoon salt
¼ teaspoon pepper
beaten egg to glaze**

*Jelly:*
**1 tablespoon gelatine
250 ml (1 cup) chicken or pork stock
salt
freshly ground black pepper**

Prepare pastry according to directions in recipe.

*Filling:* Cut pork into small pieces and mix with stock, sage, salt and pepper.

*To finish pie:* Roll two-thirds of pastry out to a round 30 cm (12 inches) in diameter. Mould pastry over an upturned, floured, straight-sided pot, 12 cm (5 inches) in diameter, pressing firmly to the sides and keeping edge level. Cut a double thickness of greaseproof paper to fit round the pie. Wrap paper round pastry and secure with string. Stand in refrigerator or a cool place until pastry is firm. Turn pot over and carefully ease it away from the pastry case, twisting gently to loosen, then stand on a baking tray. Place filling into pastry case, packing it down well to hold the shape of the pie. Roll out remaining pastry to a round large enough to cover the pie. Brush edge of pie with cold water, place round of pastry on top and press edges together to seal. Trim surplus pastry off with kitchen scissors. Cut a cross in the centre of the pie with a sharp knife and fold back the four pieces. Brush top of pie with beaten egg. Roll out pastry trimmings and cut out four leaves and make a rose. Place rose and leaves in centre of the pie to fill the hole. Brush decoration with beaten egg. Bake in a hot oven at 200°C (400°F) for 30 minutes, reduce to 180°C (350°F) and bake for a further 1¼-1½ hours. Remove paper and leave pie to cool.

*Jelly:* Dissolve gelatine in 3 tablespoons stock in a hot water bath (a bowl over a saucepan of hot water). Add remaining stock and season to taste with salt and pepper. Leave to cool. With a sharp, pointed knife, remove decoration from top of pork pie, and pour cooled jelly into pie through a funnel. Replace pastry decoration and leave pie until jelly is set. Serve pork pie cold with salad.

**Note:** A game pie tin may be used for this pie also, in which case place 4 hard-boiled eggs in the centre of the filling.

# Pork and Apple Pies

*Makes 4.*

**375 g (1 quantity) hot water crust pastry
(see page 14)**

*Filling:*
**1 onion, sliced
1 green apple, peeled, cored and sliced
60 g (2 tablespoons) butter or margarine
2 teaspoons salt
1 teaspoon chopped fresh or dried sage
¼ teaspoon ground allspice
2 rashers bacon, rinded and finely chopped
375 g (12 oz) minced pork shoulder
beaten egg to glaze**

*Pastry:* Make pastry according to directions in recipe. Divide pastry into four equal quantities and shape dough into balls, wrap each in a piece of greaseproof paper and allow to rest at room temperature for 20-30 minutes.

*Filling:* In a heavy-based frying pan, gently fry sliced onion and apple in butter over a medium heat for 8-10 minutes or until tender. Sprinkle with 1 teaspoon salt, ½ teaspoon sage and ¼ teaspoon ground allspice. Remove from heat and allow to cool. Chop bacon in a food processor, add minced pork, remaining 1 teaspoon salt and ½ teaspoon sage and mix together.

*To finish pies:* Take one ball of pastry, cut off one-third and reserve it. Remove the top and bottom of a 185 g tuna can, about 8 cm (3 inches) in diameter. Lightly grease inside of can and stand on a lightly greased baking tray. Carefully press out remaining two-thirds of pastry and gently fit it into the can. Press pastry across bottom and mould up sides of can. Keep working pastry up sides of can until it stands 1 cm (½ inch) above the edge of rim. Using a quarter of onion mixture and a quarter of pork mixture, fill pastry case with alternate layers of mixtures. Roll out reserved third of pastry on a lightly floured board until 3 mm (⅛ inch) thick and cut out a round with a 9 cm (3½ inch) fluted cutter. Brush edge of round with beaten egg and invert over pastry case, pressing it on firmly. Turn can over onto a plate, gently push pie through can and invert pie back onto a baking tray. Make a round steam vent in centre with a skewer and brush top and sides with beaten egg. Make three more pies in the same way. Bake pies towards the top of a hot oven at 200°C (400°F) for 30 minutes, reduce temperature to 180°C (350°F) and bake for a further 30 minutes. Transfer to a wire cooling tray and leave to cool. Serve pork pies cold with salad.

**Note:** The pork shoulder can be minced in a food processor. Cut pork into 5 cm (2 inch) cubes and mix for 1 minute with the double bladed knife. The pork may also be minced with a Kenwood mincer attachment.

# Maltese Timpana Pie

*Serves 6-8.*

**375 g (1½ quantities) puff, rough puff or flaky pastry (see pages 15, 16)**

*Filling:*
**185 g (1¼ cups) macaroni, cooked until just tender**
**1 onion, finely chopped**
**2 rashers bacon, rinded and finely chopped**
**2 tablespoons olive oil**
**125 g (4 oz) beef topside, finely minced**
**125 g (4 oz) lean pork, finely minced**
**125 g (4 oz) lamb's fry, finely chopped**
**1 lamb's kidney, finely chopped**
**1 x 140 g can tomato paste**
**3 tablespoons water**
**2 teaspoons sugar**
**salt**
**freshly ground black pepper**
**1 egg, lightly beaten**
**150 ml (approx. ⅔ cup) milk**
**185 g (1½ cups) Parmesan cheese**
**1 set brains, blanched, skinned and thinly sliced**
**2 hard-boiled eggs, chopped**
**60 g (2 oz) cooked ham, finely chopped**
**beaten egg for glazing**

Prepare pastry according to recipe and chill well.

*Filling:* Cook macaroni according to instructions on packet. Chop onion and bacon together in a food processor. Heat oil in a large heavy-based frying pan, add onion and bacon and cook lightly until onion is soft and transparent. Cut beef and pork into 5 cm (2 inch) cubes and mince in a food processor or with a Kenwood mincer attachment. Chop lamb's fry and kidney in a food processor. Add beef, pork, lamb's fry and kidney to frying pan and cook quickly until evenly browned. Add tomato paste, water, sugar and salt and pepper to taste. Cover and simmer gently for approx. 35-45 minutes, or until meat is cooked. Allow mixture to cool a little, then add the beaten egg, milk, Parmesan cheese and approx. a third of the cooked macaroni.

*To finish pie:* Prepare a deep 18 cm (7 inch) cake tin by placing a circle of greaseproof paper in the base. Roll out two-thirds of the pastry to a circle large enough to line the base and sides of the cake tin. Lift pastry into tin and cut out four small wedges of pastry, opposite each other so that you can mould the pastry neatly to fit the tin. Roll out remaining one-third of pastry into a round large enough to cover the top with approx. 2.5 cm (1 inch) border. Trim off about 1 cm (½ inch) of the excess pastry in one long, neat strip. Glaze underside of pastry with cold water, secure one end of strip onto pastry on edge of tin and make a complete circle with pastry strip and secure at join by pressing together gently. Place another third of the macaroni in pastry case and cover with a layer of half the meat mixture, followed by a layer of half the prepared brains, eggs and ham (chopped in a food processor or blender). Repeat this process of layers once more. Glaze underside edge of pastry lid with cold water and cover pie with it. Crimp or fork edges and if any scraps of pastry remain, cut out a Maltese cross and place in centre. Glaze pie well with beaten egg. Bake in centre of a hot oven at 200°C (400°F) for 30-40 minutes or until pastry is cooked and golden brown. Serve hot with a tossed green salad.

# Mexican Mince Pie

*Serves 6.*

**375 g (1½ quantities) short crust pastry
(see page 11)**

*Filling:*
**1 onion, finely chopped
1 red pepper, seeded and finely chopped
500 g (1 lb) finely minced beef
1 tablespoon oil
1 x 300 g can kidney beans
1 teaspoon chilli powder
1 teaspoon salt
2 tomatoes, peeled and chopped
few drops of Tabasco sauce
beaten egg for glazing**

Prepare pastry according to recipe and chill for at least 30 minutes.

*Filling:* Prepare onion, red pepper and beef in a food processor. Gently fry onion, pepper and beef in heated oil in a large frying pan until browned. Remove from heat and stir in all remaining ingredients except egg.

*To finish pie:* Roll half pastry out thinly to a round and line a 23 cm (9 inch) round pie plate. Place filling into pastry case and smooth the top. Roll remaining pastry out to a round to fit top of pie. Brush rim of pastry case with cold water. Lift remaining round of pastry onto a rolling pin and unroll over the pie dish. Seal, trim, flake and flute edge. Decorate pie by marking into segments. Brush top of pie with beaten egg. Stand pie on a baking tray and bake towards the top of a hot oven at 200°C (400°F) for 30 minutes, then lower heat to 180°C (350°F) and bake for a further 15 minutes. Serve hot with buttered squash or zucchini.

# Australian Meat Pies

*Serves 4.*

**250 g (1 quantity) short crust pastry (see page 11)**

*Filling:*
**1 onion, finely chopped
30 g (1 tablespoon) butter, margarine or oil
250 g (8 oz) minced beef
1 tablespoon plain flour
3 tablespoons tomato sauce
1 tablespoon Worcestershire sauce**

**4 tablespoons water
pinch of salt
⅛ teaspoon pepper
beaten egg to glaze**

Prepare pastry according to recipe and chill well.

*Filling:* Chop onion in a blender or a food processor. Heat butter in a heavy-based pan and gently fry onion for 5 minutes. Mince beef in a food processor or with a Kenwood mincer attachment, add to onion and stir over heat until browned. Stir in flour and cook gently for 1 minute. Add sauces, water, salt and pepper and stir until mixture comes to the boil. Remove from heat and cool.

*To finish pies:* Roll pastry out thinly on a lightly floured board and cut out four rounds large enough to line four individual 10 cm (4 inch) pie tins. Line tins, prick base of pastry cases, and chill well. Divide filling between the four pie tins. Cut four rounds out of the remaining pastry and cover pies, sealing edges together neatly. Decorate pies with pastry trimmings and make a vent in the centre of each with a skewer. Brush pies with beaten egg. Stand pie tins on a baking tray and bake towards the top of a hot oven at 220°C (425°F) for 20 minutes. Serve pies hot with tomato sauce for a snack or serve with vegetables for a meal.

# Sausage and Leek Pies

*Makes 6.*

**375 g (1½ quantities) short crust pastry
(see page 11)**

*Filling:*
**3 cups chopped leeks
125 g (½ cup) butter or margarine
250 g (8 oz) pork sausage meat
1 tablespoon oil
½ teaspoon dried sage
salt and pepper
60 g (½ cup) grated Gruyére cheese
1 egg, beaten
125 ml (½ cup) cream
beaten egg to glaze**

Prepare pastry according to recipe and chill well for at least 30 minutes.

*Filling:* Chop leeks in a food processor then sauté gently in butter in a large heavy covered pan for approx. 15 minutes. Fry sausage meat in oil in a second pan until browned, stirring occasionally. Add sautéed leeks, sage and salt and pepper to taste. Mix together, then leave to cool.

*To finish pies:* Roll pastry out thinly and cut out six rounds large enough to line six individual 10 cm (4 inch) pie tins. Line tins, prick bottom of pastry, then chill well. Sprinkle half cheese over the bottom of the pastry cases. Cover with sausage and leek mixture. Beat egg with cream and pour over the sausage filling, then sprinkle remaining cheese on top. Cut six rounds out of the remaining pastry and cover pies, sealing edges well. Decorate pies with pastry trimmings and make a vent in the centre of each with either a skewer or a pointed knife. Brush pies with beaten egg. Stand pie tins on a baking tray and bake pies at the top of a hot oven at 220°C (425°F) for 20 minutes. Serve pies hot with vegetables for a meal or serve for a snack.

# Bacon and Egg Pie

*Serves 6-8.*

**250 g (1 quantity) puff, rough puff or flaky pastry (see pages 15, 16)**

**Filling:**
**8 thin rashers streaky bacon**
**4 eggs**
**300 ml (1 jar/carton) cream, lightly whipped**
**salt and white pepper**

Prepare pastry according to recipe and chill well.

*Filling:* Remove rind and any bones from bacon and cut into 2.5 cm (1 inch) pieces with kitchen scissors. Beat eggs together in a bowl and stir in the cream. Season to taste with salt and pepper.

*To finish pie:* Divide pastry into two-thirds and one-third. Roll out two-thirds to a round on a lightly floured surface and line a 23 cm (9 inch) diameter, round pie plate. Prick the base with a fork. Sprinkle bacon pieces over base of pie and pour egg mixture over. Roll out the rest of the pastry to fit over the pie. Cover pie with pastry, press edges together, then trim and decorate edge. Make a small hole in the middle of the pastry lid to allow steam to escape during cooking. Place pie on a

baking tray and bake in a hot oven at 220°C (425°F) for 15 minutes, then reduce to a moderately hot oven at 190°C (375°F) for 30 minutes until pie is golden brown. Serve pie hot as a main course with vegetables, or cold with salad. It is excellent for picnics and packed lunches.

# CHICKEN AND RABBIT PIES

Chicken pies with their tender tempting fillings and rabbit pies with their robust flavour, are always popular pies to serve when entertaining friends to dinner.
Many of the ingredients used in these pie fillings can be prepared quickly in either a blender or food processor.
The pies which follow are covered by a variety of pastries including low cholesterol pastry, sour cream pastry, choux pastry, rough puff and phyllo pastries.

## Tips

Keep rolling pin constantly lightly floured.

When covering a pie, lift the pastry over a rolling pin and unroll over the top of the filling in the pie dish.

A narrow strip of pastry placed on top of the rim of the pie dish, under the pastry cover, gives an attractive edge to a pie. This edge is flaked and scalloped to seal the pastries together.

Never glaze the flaked edge of decorated pies as this prevents the edge rising during baking.

# Chicken and Mushroom Pie

*Serves 4-6.*

**185 g (1 quantity) one stage or low cholesterol short crust pastry (see page 11)**

*Filling:*
**1.5 kg (3 lb) dressed chicken**
**1 onion, coarsely chopped**
**1 bouquet garni**
**60 g (2 tablespoons) butter or margarine**
**250 g (8 oz) button mushrooms**
**2 tablespoons plain flour**
**300 ml (1¼ cups) chicken stock**
**1 tablespoon parsley sprigs**
**salt and white pepper**
**4 tablespoons cream**
**2 tablespoons dry white wine**
**beaten egg to glaze**

Prepare pastry according to recipe and chill well.

*Filling:* Place the chicken in a large pan with the onion (chopped in a food processor), bouquet garni and sufficient cold water to cover. Cover pan and bring slowly to the boil, then simmer until chicken is tender, about 1 hour. Remove chicken from stock and leave to cool. Heat butter in a heavy-based saucepan and gently fry mushrooms. Remove mushrooms from pan, stir in flour and stock, then pour into a blender. Blend at speed 5 for 15 seconds, then return to saucepan, and bring to the boil, over a medium heat, stirring continuously. Add mushrooms, parsley (chopped in a blender or food processor), salt and pepper to taste, cream and wine. Remove chicken meat from carcase, remove skin and cut chicken meat into bite-sized pieces.

*To finish pie:* Place chicken meat in a 1 litre oval pie dish in layers, alternating with the mushroom sauce, and leave to cool. Roll pastry out on a lightly floured board to an oval shape 4cm (1½ inches) bigger than pie dish and cut out an oval large enough to cover pie. Cut out 1 cm (½ inch) strips from remaining pastry and place on rim of pie dish, previously brushed with cold water. Brush strip of pastry with more cold water then cover with oval shape of pastry. Seal, trim, flake and scallop edges, and make a slit at either end of pie to allow steam to escape.

Make a rose and leaves from pastry scraps and place on centre of pie. Brush pastry (not flaked edges) with beaten egg. Place pie on a baking tray and bake towards the top of a hot oven at 200°C (400°F) for 25-35 minutes or until pastry is cooked and well browned. Serve hot with buttered green beans and new potatoes.

# Homestead Chicken Pie

*Serves 6.*
**250 g (1 quantity) rough puff pastry (see page 15)**

*Filling:*
**½ cup diced carrot**
**½ cup diced potato**
**½ cup diced turnip**
**½ cup chopped green beans**
**125 g (4 oz) button mushrooms, sliced**
**60 g (2 tablespoons) butter**
**3 cups cooked cubed chicken**
**½ teaspoon dried thyme**
**salt**
**freshly ground black pepper**

*Velouté sauce:*
**1 tablespoon finely chopped onion**
**90 g (3 tablespoons) butter**
**3 tablespoons plain flour**
**750 ml (3 cups) chicken stock, use stock cubes**
**¼ teaspoon salt**
**white pepper**
**beaten egg for glazing**

Make pastry according to recipe and chill well.

*Filling:* In a small pan of boiling, salted water, boil carrot, potato, turnip and green beans for 5-10 minutes, or until just tender. Drain in a colander and refresh them under running cold water. In a heavy-based frying pan, gently fry mushrooms (sliced in a food processor) in butter over a medium heat for 5 minutes. Place chicken in a mixing bowl and add all prepared vegetables.

*Velouté sauce:* Gently fry onion (previously chopped in a blender or food processor) in the butter in a saucepan until soft but not brown. Stir in flour and cook roux over a low heat, stirring continuously, for 3 minutes. Remove saucepan from heat and pour in chicken stock. Return to heat and bring to the boil, stirring continuously. Increase heat to medium and simmer

sauce for 15 minutes. Stir in salt and pepper to taste. Pour sauce over chicken and vegetables and mix gently.

*To finish pie:* Place filling in a 1 litre (4 cup) oval pie dish or casserole and leave to cool. Roll pastry out on a lightly floured board to an oval shape and cover pie as for Chicken and Mushroom Pie (see page 28). Brush pastry (not flaked edges) with beaten egg. Place pie on a baking tray and bake towards the top of a hot oven at 220°C (425°F) for 20-30 minutes or until pastry is golden. Serve hot with buttered green beans and silverbeet.

# Creamed Chicken Pie

*Serves 4-6.*

**250 g (1 quantity) short crust pastry (see page 11)**

*Filling:*
**125 g (½ cup) packaged cream cheese**
**2 x 60 g eggs**
**2 tablespoons finely chopped parsley**
**½ teaspoon salt**
**freshly ground black pepper**
**125 ml (½ cup) cream**
**500 g (1 lb) chopped cooked chicken**
**125 g (4 oz) button mushrooms, sliced**

Make pastry according to recipe and chill well.

*Filling:* Beat cream cheese in an electric mixer at maximum speed for 1 minute. Add eggs, parsley (chopped in a blender), salt, pepper and cream and continue to beat, gradually increasing speed from minimum to maximum, then beat at maximum for 30-40 seconds. Chop chicken in a blender or food processor, slice mushrooms in a food processor.

*To finish pie:* Roll pastry out on a lightly floured board and line a deep 20 cm (8 inch) flan tin. Spread chicken and mushrooms over base of pastry case and spoon cream cheese mixture over. Place flan tin on a baking tray and bake towards the top of a moderately hot oven at 190°C (375°F) for 30-35 minutes. Serve warm or cold, accompanied by a tossed salad.

# Plantation Chicken Pie

*Serves 6.*

**185 g (1 quantity) sour cream pastry (see page 13)**

*Filling:*
**2 onions, finely chopped**
**1 small green pepper, seeded and finely chopped**
**1 clove garlic, crushed**
**3 tablespoons olive oil**
**3 cups shredded cooked chicken**
**310 g can corn kernels, drained**
**425 g can tomatoes, drained and chopped**
**¾ cup chopped black olives, optional**
**2 teaspoons chilli powder**
**salt**
**freshly ground black pepper**
**125 g (1 cup) grated Cheddar cheese**
**beaten egg to glaze**

Make pastry according to recipe and chill well.

*Filling:* Chop onions and green pepper in a blender or food processor. In a large heavy-based frying pan, gently fry onions, green pepper and garlic in olive oil for 8-10 minutes, or until onion is soft and transparent and green pepper is tender. Add chicken, corn kernels, tomatoes, black olives (chopped in blender or food processor), chilli powder and salt and pepper to taste. Allow mixture to cool, then stir in grated cheese.

*To finish pie:* Place mixture in a 1 litre (4 cup) oval pie dish. On a lightly floured board, roll out pastry to an oval shape and cover pie as for Chicken and Mushroom Pie (see page 28). Brush pastry with lightly beaten egg. Place pie on a baking tray and bake towards the top of a hot oven at 220°C (425°F) for 25-30 minutes or until pastry is cooked and well browned. Serve hot with buttered zucchini and baby squash.

# Chicken and Sausage Pie

*Serves 4-6.*

**185 g (1 quantity) sour cream or (¾ quantity) short crust pastry (see pages 11, 13)**

*Filling:*
**250 g (8 oz) pork sausages**
**60 g (2 tablespoons) butter or margarine**
**500 g (1 lb) white onions or leeks, thinly sliced**
**250 g (8 oz) chopped cooked chicken**
**2 tablespoons plain flour**
**2 chicken stock cubes**
**500 ml (2 cups) water**
**2 tablespoons chopped parsley**
**beaten egg to glaze**

Prepare pastry according to recipe and chill well.

*Filling:* Place sausages in a pan of water, cover and bring to boil and simmer for 30 minutes. Drain sausages, cool and cut into 5 mm (¼ inch) slices. Heat 1 tablespoon butter in a heavy-based frying pan and fry onions or leeks (previously prepared in a food processor) until golden and transparent. Place fried onions in a 1 litre (4 cup) oval pie dish and add sliced sausages and chopped chicken (prepared in a food processor or blender). Melt remaining butter in a saucepan, stir in flour and cook roux gently for 2 minutes, stirring continuously. Dissolve stock cubes in water, add slowly to saucepan and bring to the boil, stirring continuously, then simmer for 2 minutes. Add parsley, chopped in a blender or food processor. Pour gravy over sausage pie filling and leave to cool.

*To finish pie:* Roll pastry out on a lightly floured board to an oval and cover pie as for Chicken and Mushroom Pie (see page 28). Brush top of pie with beaten egg, decorate with pastry leaves if desired. Place pie dish on a baking tray and bake in a hot oven at 220°C (425°F) for 30 minutes. Serve hot with buttered carrots and peas.

# Chicken and Mushroom Choux Ring

*Serves 6-8.*

**125 g (1 quantity) savoury choux pastry (see page 16)**
**2 rashers bacon**
**2 tablespoons grated Parmesan cheese**

*Filling:*
**1 tablespoon butter**
**1 small onion, finely chopped**
**250 g (8 oz) mushroom caps, quartered**

**1 tablespoon plain flour**
**250 ml (1 cup) chicken stock**
**375 g (3 cups) chopped cooked chicken**
**salt and pepper**

Prepare pastry according to recipe. Cut rind and bones off bacon rashers and chop bacon finely in either a blender or a food processor. Spoon choux pastry dough in a ring shape, 20 cm (8 inches) in diameter, on a greased baking tray. Sprinkle chopped bacon and cheese on top. Bake in a moderately hot oven at 190°C (375°F) for 30 minutes, then increase temperature to 200°C (400°F) and bake for a further 30 minutes or until firm to the touch. Split ring in two while still hot, turn oven off and return ring to oven, with door ajar and allow to dry inside a little so that choux pastry ring will retain its attractive puffed shape.

*Filling:* Heat butter in a heavy pan and gently fry onion (chopped in food processor or blender) for 2 minutes. Add mushrooms and fry for 4 minutes, stirring occasionally. Stir in flour and cook over a low heat for 1-2 minutes. Add stock and bring to the boil, stirring occasionally. Stir in chicken (chopped in food processor or blender), heat through on a low heat and season to taste with salt and pepper.

*To finish pie:* Spoon hot filling into hot choux ring, replace top and serve immediately accompanied by a tossed salad.

# Pioneer Rabbit Pie

*Serves 4.*

**250 g (1 quantity) short crust pastry (see page 11)**

**Filling:**
**2 small young rabbits, cut into joints**
**125 ml (½ cup) red wine**
**8 rashers bacon, rinded**
**½ teaspoon ground mace**
**1 teaspoon salt**
**3 tablespoons finely chopped parsley**
**3 tablespoons finely chopped chives**
**1 teaspoon dried sweet basil**
**livers of the 2 rabbits**
**4 small pickling onions, peeled**
**60 g (2 tablespoons) butter**
**beaten egg to glaze**

Prepare pastry according to recipe and chill well.

*Filling:* Marinate rabbit pieces in wine for 1-2 hours or overnight if liked. Chop 4 rashers of bacon one at a time in a blender. Combine them with mace, salt, parsley, chives, sweet basil and livers in an electric blender or food processor and mix to a smooth paste. Line the bottom of a 1 litre (4 cup) oval pie dish with the paste, place pieces of rabbit on top, then add onions. Chop another rasher of bacon and blend to a smooth paste with the butter in an electric blender or food processor. Spread paste over rabbit. Cover rabbit with remaining 3 rashers of bacon.

*To finish pie:* Roll pastry into a large oval or rectangle. Place pie dish in the centre (briefly, as this will mark pastry), then run a sharp pointed knife around the edge of the dish to determine the size and shape that you will need for the top of the pie. Then run around again with a sharp pointed knife, about 2 cm (¾ inch) around the outside of the first mark. Lift centre oval of pastry out and place aside until required. Wet rim of pie dish with cold water and lift the remaining strip of pastry onto the rim. Brush strip with cold water then place oval of pastry on top, press together gently and seal. Flake edges with a round-bladed knife and flute in 16 scallops. Make a slit at either end with a knife to allow the steam to escape and decorate top of pie with small pastry leaves made from the pastry trimmings. Glaze pastry with beaten egg. Place pie dish on a baking tray and bake at 220°C (425°F) for 15 minutes or until pastry is golden, then reduce temperature to 180°C (350°F), cover pastry with a piece of wet greaseproof paper to prevent toughening and continue baking pie for a further 45 minutes or until rabbit is tender. Serve hot with mashed pumpkin and creamed potatoes.

# Rabbit Pie

*Serves 4.*

**250 g (1 quantity) puff, rough puff or flaky
   pastry (see pages 15, 16)**

*Filling:*
**250 g (8 oz) bacon rashers, rinded and
   finely chopped
30 g (1 tablespoon) lard or dripping
1 kg (2 lb) rabbit, jointed
3 tablespoons plain flour
500 ml (2 cups) stock
125 g (4 oz) mushrooms
30 g (1 tablespoon) butter or margarine
salt and pepper
beaten egg to glaze**

Prepare pastry according to recipe and
chill well.

*Filling:* Fry bacon (chopped in food processor or blender) in a heated frying pan in
its own fat. Drain and place in a casserole.
Heat lard or dripping in pan. Coat rabbit
joints with flour and fry on all sides until
brown. Place rabbit in casserole. Add any
remaining flour to pan and cook for 1-2
minutes, stirring continuously, until golden.
Add stock and bring to the boil, stirring
continuously, then add to casserole. Cover
and cook in a moderately slow oven at
160°C (325°F) for 1½ hours or until rabbit
is tender. Leave to cool. Remove meat from
cold rabbit and place in a 1 litre (4 cup)
oval pie dish; discard bones. Fry mushrooms in butter or margarine and add to
rabbit. Pour the meat liquor over. Season
with salt and pepper.

*To finish pie:* Roll pastry out and cover and
decorate pie as directed in Pioneer Rabbit
Pie (see page 31). Glaze pie with beaten
egg. Place pie on a baking tray and bake
towards the top of a hot oven at 220°C
(425°F) for 25-35 minutes or until pastry is
cooked and golden brown. Serve hot with
buttered new potatoes and green peas.

# Choux Rabbit Fricassée

*Serves 4-6.*

**60 g (1 quantity) choux pastry (see page
   15)**

*Filling:*
**250 g (2 cups) cooked rabbit meat (1 small
   rabbit), finely chopped**

**6 pickling onions, blanched
125 g (4 oz) button mushrooms, halved and
   sautéed in butter
45 g (1½ tablespoons) butter or margarine
3 tablespoons plain flour
300 ml (approx. 1¼ cups) milk
salt
freshly ground black pepper
¼ teaspoon mustard powder**

Make pastry according to recipe. Spoon
into a clean dry piping bag fitted with a
1 cm (½ inch) plain tube.

*Filling:* Place cooked rabbit (chopped in
blender or food processor), onions and
mushrooms in a bowl. Melt butter in a
heavy-based saucepan over a medium
heat. Add flour and cook the roux, stirring
continuously, for 1-2 minutes. Remove from
heat, gradually stir in milk, then return to
heat and bring to the boil, stirring continuously, and simmer for 1 minute. Season
sauce to taste with salt and pepper and
add mustard powder. Pour sauce over
rabbit mixture and mix gently.

*To finish pie:* Place filling in a 1 litre
(4 cup) oval pie dish. Pipe choux pastry
over the top, starting at the edge of the pie
dish and working round into the centre.
Stand pie dish on a baking tray and bake
towards the top of a hot oven at 200°C
(400°F) for 30-35 minutes, then at moderately hot, 190°C (375°F) for 15-20 minutes
or until pastry is golden and puffed. Serve
immediately with green peas and buttered
carrots.

# Turkey Phyllo Pie

*Serves 10.*

**16 sheets phyllo pastry
185 g (¾ cup) butter**

*Filling:*
**2 tablespoons olive oil
1 cup finely chopped shallots
500 g (4 cups) cooked turkey or chicken
¼ cup chopped mint or parsley
1 teaspoon ground cinnamon
¼ teaspoon ground nutmeg
1 teaspoon salt
freshly ground black pepper
60 g (½ cup) pine nuts
60 g (2 tablespoons) butter**

Unwrap phyllo pastry and stack between two clean, cold, damp teatowels. Melt butter in a pan over a low heat.

*Filling:* Heat olive oil in a large frying pan and gently fry shallots until soft but not brown. Mince turkey with the Kenwood mincer attachment or in a food processor. Add minced turkey to frying pan and stir over heat until lightly browned. Drain oil from pan. Stir in mint (chopped in blender or food processor), spices, salt and pepper. Brown pine nuts in butter and add to turkey mixture. Leave filling to cool to lukewarm.

*To finish pie:* Brush a lamington tin with melted butter. Carefully remove one sheet of phyllo pastry at a time, brush with melted butter and layer into the lamington tin, allowing pastry to come up sides and overlap the edges. Repeat this three times. Spread one-third of the turkey filling over the layered phyllo. Repeat with four layers of buttered phyllo pastry, then one-third of the turkey filling, repeat once again, until all the turkey mixture is used. Finally, top with four layers of buttered phyllo pastry. Press gently around edge, then with kitchen scissors cut pastry off at rim of pan. Bake in a moderately hot oven at 190°C (375°F) for 45 minutes or until pastry is puffed and golden. Serve hot or warm, cut in diamonds, accompanied by a green salad or ratatouille.

**Note:** An unusual recipe for using up your leftover Christmas turkey. Cut into smaller pieces and serve as a delicious party savoury.

# FISH PIES

When the fisherman in your family comes home with a very mixed catch of fish, the best thing you can make with them is a delicious fish pie. Fish pies are also very economical family meals because you can choose from the cheapest fish at the markets and turn 500 g of fish into a delicious dish which will serve four people. Many of these fish pies are topped with creamy mashed potato and the Kenwood potato peeler gets rid of the messy job of peeling them while the K beater takes the hard work out of creaming them. Good fishing to you.

# Tips

Use up your left-over mashed potatoes for covering a fish pie.

Make a sauce the foolproof way by mixing the milk, flour and butter altogether in the Kenwood blender, then pour into a saucepan and bring to the boil, stirring continuously.

## Crunchy Fish Pie

*Serves 4-6.*

**250 g (1 quantity) rough puff or flaky pastry (see pages 15, 16)**

*Filling:*
**500 g (1 lb) white fish fillets, bream or similar**
**¼ cup lemon juice**
**1 medium onion, chopped**
**2 stalks celery, chopped**
**1 eating apple, peeled, cored and chopped**
**60 g (2 tablespoons) butter or margarine**
**1½ tablespoons plain flour**
**325 ml (1⅓ cups) evaporated milk**
**1 tablespoon chopped parsley**
**⅛ teaspoon grated or ground nutmeg**
**⅛ teaspoon mustard powder**
**1½ teaspoons salt**
**¼ teaspoon cayenne pepper**
**evaporated milk to glaze**

Prepare pastry according to recipe and chill well.

*Filling:* Skin fish and remove bones. Poach fish in lemon juice for 5 minutes, set aside. Prepare onion, celery and apple in a blender or food processor, then gently fry in butter in a saucepan until soft but not brown. Sprinkle in the flour. Gradually add evaporated milk, then bring to the boil, stirring constantly. Fold in flaked fish, fish liquor and seasonings.

*To finish pie:* Spoon fish mixture into a pie dish. Roll out pastry 5 mm (¼ inch) thick, cover dish, trim, seal and decorate edges as for Steak and Kidney Pie (see page 22). Brush pastry with evaporated milk. Place pie on a baking tray and bake in a hot oven at 220°C (425°F) for 15-20 minutes, or until pastry is golden and cooked. Serve hot with green beans and sautéed tomatoes.

## Fisherman's Pie

*Serves 4.*

*Filling:*
**500 g (1 lb) white fish fillets, bream, jewfish or flathead**
**300 ml (1¼ cups) milk**
**1 teaspoon salt**
**¼ teaspoon white pepper**
**1 bay leaf**
**30 g (1 tablespoon) butter or margarine**

**2 tablespoons plain flour**
**60 g (½ cup) Cheddar cheese, grated**
**2 hard-boiled eggs, chopped**

*Topping:*
**750 g (1½ lb) potatoes**
**30 g (1 tablespoon) butter or margarine**
**3 tablespoons milk**

*Filling:* Place fish in a shallow, greased baking dish. Pour milk over and sprinkle with salt, pepper and a bay leaf. Cover and cook in a moderate oven at 180°C (350°F) for 15-20 minutes or until fish is cooked—it will flake easily and should turn white. Drain liquor off fish and reserve. Flake fish and discard bones and skin. Place fish liquor, butter and flour in a blender and mix until smooth. Pour into a saucepan and bring to the boil, stirring continuously. Stir flaked fish, cheese (grated in a food processor) and hard-boiled eggs (chopped in a blender or food processor) into sauce. Adjust seasoning to taste.

*Topping:* Peel potatoes in the Kenwood potato peeler attachment, then boil in salted water until tender. Drain well. Mash in an electric mixer at minimum speed for 10 seconds, add butter and milk and beat at speed 5 for 20 seconds or until smooth and creamy.

*To finish pie:* Pour filling into a buttered pie dish or casserole. Spread potatoes over filling and fork neatly. Place on a baking tray and bake in a hot oven at 200°C (400°F) for 15 minutes or until golden brown and hot. Serve hot with baked tomatoes and green peas or beans.

**Variation:** Substitute a 105 g can shrimps for the cheese and eggs.

# Smoked Fish Pie

*Serves 4.*

*Filling:*
**250 g (8 oz) smoked cod or haddock**
**250 g (8 oz) white fish fillets, flathead or**
**   jewfish**
**250 ml (1 cup) milk**
**125 ml (½ cup) water**
**30 g (1 tablespoon) butter or margarine**
**2 tablespoons plain flour**
**1 teaspoon vinegar**
**2 teaspoons capers**
**1 tablespoon parsley sprigs**

**½ teaspoon salt**
**¼ teaspoon white pepper**
**2 hard-boiled eggs, chopped**

*Topping:*
**750 g (1½ lb) potatoes**
**30 g (1 tablespoon) butter or margarine**
**3 tablespoons milk**

*Filling:* Place fish in a shallow, greased baking dish. Pour milk and water over, cover and cook in a moderate oven at 180°C (350°F) for 15-20 minutes or until fish is cooked. Drain liquor off fish and measure and reserve 1½ cups. Flake fish with a fork and discard skin and bones. Place reserved fish liquor, butter, flour, vinegar, capers, parsley sprigs, salt and pepper in a blender and mix at maximum speed for 30 seconds. Pour sauce mixture into a saucepan and bring to the boil, stirring continuously, then simmer for 2 minutes. Add flaked fish and hard-boiled eggs (chopped in a blender or food processor) and mix gently.

*Topping:* Peel potatoes in the Kenwood potato peeler attachment, then boil in salted water, drain and mash well in electric mixer. Add butter and milk and beat until smooth and creamy.

*To finish pie:* Pour filling into a buttered pie dish or casserole. Spread potatoes over filling and fork neatly. Place on a baking tray and bake in a hot oven at 200°C (400°F) for 30 minutes or until golden brown and hot. Serve hot with broccoli or spinach and grilled tomatoes.

# Lemon Fish Pie

*Serves 4.*

**Filling:**
**500 g (1 lb) flathead or murray cod fillets**
**2 onions, finely chopped**
**2 carrots, finely chopped**
**300 ml (1¼ cups) milk**
**seasoned salt**
**lemon pepper**
**30 g (1 tablespoon) butter or margarine**
**2 tablespoons plain flour**
**juice of 1 lemon**

**Topping:**
**750 g (1½ lb) potatoes**
**30 g (1 tablespoon) butter or margarine**
**3 tablespoons milk**
**potato chips, lightly crushed for sprinkling**
**lemon and parsley for garnish**

*Filling:* Place the fish fillets in a shallow, greased baking dish with the onions and carrots (chopped in a blender or food processor). Pour milk over and sprinkle with seasoned salt and lemon pepper. Cover and cook in a moderate oven at 180°C (350°F) for 15 minutes, or until fish is cooked—it turns white. Carefully drain off the liquor into a measuring cup and make up to 300 ml with extra milk if necessary. Remove skin and bones from fish and flake the fish flesh with a fork. Place fish liquor, butter and flour in a blender and mix until smooth. Pour into a saucepan and bring to the boil, stirring continuously. Simmer for 2-3 minutes or until the sauce has thickened. Stir the onion, carrot, fish and lemon juice into the sauce.

*Topping:* Peel potatoes in the Kenwood potato peeler attachment then boil in salted water till tender, drain and mash well in an electric mixer. Add butter and milk and beat well until smooth and creamy.

*To finish pie:* Pour filling into a buttered pie dish or casserole. Place potato in a large piping bag fitted with a star pipe and pipe the potato around the edge of the dish. Sprinkle crushed potato chips over the top. Place pie dish on a baking tray and bake in a moderate oven at 180°C (350°F) for 15-20 minutes or until hot. Garnish with lemon slices and sprigs of parsley. Serve hot with baked or grilled halved tomatoes and green peas.

# Salmon Puff Pie

*Serves 4-6.*

**250 g (1 quantity) puff, rough puff or flaky**
**pastry (see pages 15, 16)**

**Filling:**
**60 g (2 tablespoons) butter**
**125 g (4 oz) button mushrooms, sliced**
**1 small green pepper, seeded and sliced**
**3 tablespoons plain flour**
**300 ml (approx. 1¼ cups) chicken stock,**
**use stock cubes**
**125 ml (½ cup) milk**
**460 g can salmon, drained and flaked**
**1 tablespoon cream**
**salt**
**freshly ground black pepper**
**beaten egg to glaze**

Make pastry according to recipe and refrigerate until required.

*Filling:* Melt butter in a heavy-based saucepan and gently fry mushrooms and green pepper (both prepared in a food processor) for 2-3 minutes. Transfer vegetables with a slotted spoon to drain on absorbent kitchen paper towels. Stir flour into remaining butter in pan and cook roux for 2-3 minutes. Remove from heat, add stock and milk gradually, stirring continuously. Return to heat and bring to the boil. continuously, then simmer for 1 minute. Add salmon, mushrooms, green pepper and cream. Season to taste with salt and pepper.

*To finish pie:* Pour filling into a 23 cm (9 inch) round pie plate and allow to cool. Roll out pastry 5 mm (¼ inch) thick and cut out rounds with a 5-8 cm (2-3 inch) plain cutter. Place circles of pastry, overlapping, over filling in pie plate. Rest in refrigerator for 15-20 minutes. Carefully glaze pastry (not cut edges) with beaten egg. Place pie plate on a baking tray and bake towards the top of a hot oven at 220°C (425°F) for 20-25 minutes or until pastry has risen and is golden brown. Serve hot with buttered fennel and green beans.

Salmon Puff Pie and Fisherman's Pie
*(see above and page 34)*

# Italian Tuna Pie

*Serves 6.*

**250 g (1 quantity) short crust or one-stage short crust pastry (see pages 11, 12)**

*Filling:*
**2 tablespoons olive oil**
**1 onion, chopped**
**3 carrots, thinly sliced**
**1 clove garlic, crushed**
**125 ml (½ cup) tomato sauce**
**1 teaspoon anchovy paste**
**1 teaspoon dried oregano**
**425 g can tomatoes**
**2 tablespoons plain flour**
**185 g can tuna, drained and flaked**
**2 tablespoons sliced olives**
**125 g (1 cup) grated Parmesan cheese**
**salt and pepper**
**parsley sprigs for garnish**

Prepare pastry according to recipe and chill well.

*Filling:* Heat oil in a large, heavy frying pan and gently fry onion, carrot (both prepared in a food processor) and garlic for 5 minutes or until vegetables are soft. Stir in tomato sauce, anchovy paste and oregano. Drain tomatoes, reserve liquid and slice tomatoes. Blend flour smoothly with tomato liquid, stir into frying pan and bring to the boil, stirring continuously. Remove pan from heat and stir in sliced tomatoes, tuna, olives and half the Parmesan cheese. Season to taste with salt and pepper and leave to cool.

*To finish pie:* Roll out pastry on a lightly floured board to a round and line a 23 cm (9 inch) round pie plate. Press pastry into shape, trim and decorate edge and prick base. Chill in refrigerator for 15 minutes. Pour filling into pastry case and sprinkle remaining cheese over the top. Place pie dish on a baking tray and bake in a moderately hot oven at 190°C (375°F) for 30 minutes or until cooked. Serve pie hot with a tossed salad.

# Oyster Pie

*Serves 4-6.*

*Filling:*
**4 dozen oysters (in jars)**
**½ cup chopped celery**
**½ cup chopped green pepper**
**90 g (3 tablespoons) butter or margarine**
**4 tablespoons plain flour**
**625 ml (2½ cups) milk**
**salt and pepper**

*Topping:*
**750 g (1½ lb) potatoes**
**30 g (1 tablespoon) butter or margarine**
**3 tablespoons milk**

*Filling:* Gently simmer oysters in the oyster liquor for 5 minutes, drain well. Chop celery and green pepper in a blender or food processor, then gently fry in butter in a heavy-based saucepan. Add flour and stir to make a roux, then cook for 1 minute, stirring continuously. Stir in milk and bring to the boil, stirring continuously. Add oysters to sauce and season to taste with salt and pepper.

*Topping:* Peel potatoes in a Kenwood potato peeler attachment. Cook potatoes in boiling, salted water until tender, 20-30 minutes, drain well. Mash in an electric mixer at minimum speed for 10 seconds, add butter and milk and beat at speed 5 for 20 seconds or until smooth and creamy.

*To finish pie:* Pour filling into a buttered pie dish. Place creamed potato in a large piping bag with a star pipe and pipe rosettes or scrolls on top of filling. Place on a baking tray and bake in a hot oven at 200°C (400°F) until hot and golden brown, about 15 minutes. Serve hot with a tomato salad.

Hunza Pie and Ratatouille Pie
*(see pages 43, 44)*

# Russian Fish Pie

*Serves 4.*

**250 g (1 quantity) rough puff or flaky
pastry (see pages 15, 16)**

*Filling:*
**500 g (1 lb) white fish fillets, bream or
flathead
milk, approx. 300 ml
30 g (1 tablespoon) butter or margarine
2 tablespoons plain flour
salt and pepper
1 tablespoon chopped parsley
2 hard-boiled eggs, chopped
beaten egg to glaze
parsley sprigs for garnish**

Make pastry according to recipe and chill
well.

*Filling:* Wash and trim fish, place skin side
down in a greased baking dish and pour
sufficient milk over to cover the bottom of
the dish. Cover and cook fish in a moderate
oven at 180°C (350°F) for 15-20 minutes or
until flesh is white and will lift easily from
the bone and skin. Drain off fish liquor and
make up to 300 ml with milk. Flake fish
with a fork, remove and discard skin and
bones. Place fish liquor, butter and flour in
a blender and mix until smooth. Pour into a
saucepan and bring to the boil, stirring
continuously. Season to taste with salt and
pepper and stir in chopped parsley (prepared in a blender or food processor).
Mix flaked fish with 3 tablespoons parsley
sauce, chopped hard-boiled eggs (prepared in blender or food processor) and
salt and pepper to taste. Cover remaining
sauce with wet greaseproof paper to avoid
lumps when reheated later.

*To finish pie:* Roll pastry out to a 23-25 cm
(9-10 inch) square. Turn over so that rolled
side is downwards and trim edges straight
with a long, sharp knife. Lift pastry onto
rolling pin and place on a large baking tray
so that the points of the pastry overlap the
sides of the tin. Place fish filling in a neat
square in the centre of the pastry. Brush
edges of pastry with beaten egg. Lift each
corner up over the centre of the fish and
press the moistened edges together to seal
well. Flake sealed edges if desired. This
makes a square pastry envelope. Brush pie
with beaten egg, but do not glaze sealed
edges or they will not flake. Roll pastry
trimmings out, cut into strips 1 cm (½ inch)
wide and cut diagonally to make diamond-
shaped leaves. Mark leaves with veins and
place on the pie between the joins. Brush
leaves with beaten egg. Bake pie in a hot
oven at 220°C (425°F) for 15 minutes or
until pastry is risen and golden brown.
Reduce oven temperature to moderately
slow at 160°C (325°F) and continue cooking for a further 20-30 minutes. Serve pie
hot, garnished with a sprig of parsley,
accompanied with reserved parsley sauce,
buttered new potatoes and broad beans or
peas.

# Salmon Tartare Pie

*Serves 6.*

*Filling:*
**30 g (1 oz) packet tartare sauce mix
2 tablespoons lemon juice
300 ml (1 jar/carton) sour cream
460 g can salmon, drained and flaked
¼ cup chopped shallots
3 eggs, lightly beaten**

*Topping:*
**750 g (1½ lb) potatoes
30 g (1 tablespoon) butter
3 tablespoons milk
¼ teaspoon lemon pepper
90 g (¾ cup) Cheddar cheese, grated**

*Filling:* Place tartare sauce mix in a bowl,
add lemon juice and blend well. Stir in sour
cream and refrigerate for 30 minutes. Combine salmon with shallots (chopped in a
blender or food processor), eggs and
tartare sauce mixture.

*Topping:* Peel potatoes in Kenwood potato
peeler attachment. Place in a pan of
boiling salted water to cover, and boil for
15-20 minutes or until tender when tested
with a skewer. Drain potatoes and mash in
an electric mixer at minimum speed for 10
seconds. Add butter, milk and lemon
pepper and beat at speed 5 for 20 seconds
or until smooth and creamy.

*To finish pie:* Butter a 2 litre (8 cup) pie
dish or casserole and spread half the
potato mixture over the base. Pour filling
over potatoes, then spread remaining
mashed potatoes over the top, fork attractively and sprinkle with grated cheese.
Place pie dish on a baking tray and bake
in a moderate oven at 180°C (350°F) for
50 minutes. Serve hot with creamed
spinach and baked tomatoes.

# Rosy Fish Pie

*Serves 4.*

**Filling:**
**500 g (1 lb) flathead fillets, skinned**
**1 small onion**
**2 rashers bacon**
**30 g (1 tablespoon) butter or margarine**
**2 tablespoons plain flour**
**½ x 425 g can tomatoes**
**salt**
**freshly ground black pepper**

**Topping:**
**500 g (1 lb) potatoes**
**30 g (1 tablespoon) butter or margarine**
**1 tablespoon milk**

*Filling:* Cut fish into 5 cm (2 inch) cubes and remove any bones. Peel onion, remove rind from bacon and place onion and bacon in a Kenwood blender and mix at speed 5 for 5 seconds. Fry onion and bacon in butter for 5 minutes or until soft and transparent, add fish and cook gently for a further 10 minutes. Stir in the flour, tomatoes and salt and pepper to taste.

*Topping:* Peel potatoes in the Kenwood potato peeler attachment, then boil in salted water until tender, drain and mash in an electric mixer at minimum speed for 10 seconds. Add butter and milk and beat at speed 5 for 20 seconds or until smooth and creamy.

*To finish pie:* Place filling in a buttered pie dish or casserole. Cover filling with creamed potatoes, spread smooth with a spatula or palette knife, then decorate with a fork. Place pie dish on a baking tray and bake in a hot oven at 200°C (400°F) for 30-35 minutes or until pie is hot and golden brown on top. Serve hot with green beans or a green salad.

# Budget Pie

*Serves 2.*

**Filling:**
**15 g (½ tablespoon) soft margarine**
**1 tablespoon plain flour**
**125 ml (½ cup) milk**
**salt and pepper**
**185 g can tuna, flaked**
**1 tablespoon tomato sauce**

**Topping:**
**½ x 125 g packet instant mashed potato**

*Filling:* Place margarine, flour and milk together in a saucepan and bring to the boil over a medium heat, stirring continuously with a balloon-shaped whisk for 2 minutes or until thickened. Add salt and pepper to taste. Gently stir in the tuna and tomato sauce, heat through and keep warm.

*Topping:* Make mashed potato according to instructions on the packet and beat smooth with an electric hand mixer.

*To finish pie:* Pour filling into a 625 ml (2½ cup) pie dish. Spread the warm mashed potato on top and brown under a medium grill for 5 minutes. Serve hot with a green vegetable.

# Tuna Tart

*Serves 4-6.*

**Crust:**
**2 cups cooked long grain rice ( ⅔ cup raw)**
**30 g (1 tablespoon) butter or margarine, melted**
**1 onion, finely chopped**
**1 tablespoon chopped mint**

**Filling:**
**1 x 185 g can tuna**
**3 x 60 g eggs**
**375 ml can evaporated milk**
**1 small onion, finely chopped**
**125 g (1 cup) Swiss cheese, grated**
**1½ teaspoons salt**
**¼ teaspoon cayenne pepper**
**⅛ teaspoon dried marjoram (optional)**
**mint sprigs and tomato segments for garnish**

*Crust:* Combine rice, butter, onion and mint (chopped in a blender or food processor) in a bowl and mix well. Press onto sides and base of a well buttered round 23 cm (9 inch) pie or tart plate.

*Filling:* Drain tuna and flake with a fork. Beat eggs, evaporated milk, onion, cheese (grated in a food processor) and seasonings together in an electric mixer.

*To finish pie:* Place flaked tuna evenly over the rice shell. Pour egg mixture over tuna. Bake in a moderate oven at 180°C (350°F) for 40-50 minutes or until filling is set. Serve hot or cold garnished with mint sprigs and tomato segments and accompanied by a tossed salad.

# VEGETABLE PIES

A vegetable pie can make a healthy, refreshing change in your menu. If you grow your own vegetables you will find these recipes for vegetable pies most useful if not surprising, particularly when combined with nutty textured wholemeal pastry. There are also a few healthy vegetable pasties here for the school lunch box.

## Tips

Try chopping onions in the Kenwood blender—it chops a whole onion finely in 3-4 seconds at minimum speed.

If reheating a pastry-topped pie in the oven, wrap a sheet of wet greaseproof paper over the pastry to prevent it from toughening.

# Cheese and Vegetable Pasties

*Makes 6.*

**250 g (1 quantity) low cholesterol wholemeal pastry (see page 14)**

*Filling:*
**30 g (1 tablespoon) polyunsaturated margarine**
**1 onion, finely chopped**
**125 g (1 cup) curly cabbage, finely shredded**
**250 g (1 cup) sliced beans**
**1 teaspoon mustard powder**
**125 g (1 cup) pumpkin, grated**
**125 g (1 cup) Cheddar cheese, grated**
**1 teaspoon salt**
**¼ teaspoon ground black pepper**
**beaten egg to glaze**
**caraway seeds for sprinkling**

Prepare pastry according to recipe and chill well.

*Filling:* Melt margarine in a medium-sized saucepan, add onion (chopped in a blender or food processor), cabbage, beans (both prepared in the Kenwood slicer and shredder attachment or food processor) and mustard and gently fry for 5 minutes. Remove from heat, stir in pumpkin and cheese (both grated in a food processor) and season with salt and pepper.

*To finish pasties:* Roll out pastry to 3 mm (⅛ inch) thick and cut out 6 rounds using a saucer as a guide. Turn rounds over and place an equal amount of prepared filling on each one. Brush halfway around the edges with cold water. Join edges together over the top of the mixture and pinch a frill along edges. Place pasties on a greased baking tray. Brush each pastie with egg and sprinkle with caraway seeds. Bake in a hot oven at 200°C (400°F) for 10 minutes, then at 180°C (350°F) for a further 25 minutes. Serve warm with vegetables or salad or use for a packed lunch.

# Herb Pie

*Serves 6.*

**250 g (1 quantity) short crust or 185 g (1 quantity) sour cream pastry (see pages 11, 13)**

**Filling:**
**500 g (2⅔ cups) oatmeal, medium or coarse ground**
**2 onions, chopped**
**2 cooking apples, peeled, cored and chopped**
**1 small lettuce, coarsely shredded**
**500 g (1 lb) spinach or silverbeet, coarsely shredded**
**1 leek, thinly sliced**
**1 cup chopped parsley or mixed fresh herbs**
**125 g (½ cup) butter or polyunsaturated margarine**
**salt and pepper**

Prepare pastry according to recipe and chill well.

*Filling:* Place oatmeal, chopped onion and apple (prepared in a blender or food processor) into a heavy pan, add cold water to cover and bring to the boil, then cook gently until apple is tender, about 10-15 minutes. Drain well. Place prepared lettuce, spinach and leek (all prepared in the Kenwood slicer and shredder attachment) and parsley (prepared in a food processor or blender) into a heavy pan with a little water and boil for 5-7 minutes. Drain well, reserve liquor for soup or gravy. Mix lettuce mixture with oatmeal mixture and fry in heated butter or margarine for 5 minutes. Season to taste with salt and pepper.

*To finish pie:* Roll out pastry and line a 23 cm (9 inch) pie dish. Place the herb and oatmeal mixture in it. Place pie dish on a baking tray and bake in a hot oven at 220°C (425°F) for 15 minutes or until pastry is cooked. Serve hot.

# Hunza Pie

*Serves 6.*

**375 g (double quantity) wholemeal wheatgerm pastry (see page 14)**

**Filling:**
**1 kg (2 lb) potatoes, cooked**
**1 bunch spinach, approx. 1 kg (2 lb)**
**1 tablespoon kelp**
**1 teaspoon vegetable salt**
**freshly ground black pepper**
**185 g (1½ cups) Cheddar cheese, grated**

Prepare wholemeal wheatgerm pastry according to recipe and chill well.

*Filling:* Using Kenwood potato peeler attachment, peel potatoes then boil in salted water until tender. Drain well. Mash potatoes in the electric mixer using the K beater. Wash spinach and shake dry. Shred spinach finely in the Kenwood slicer and shredder attachment and add to potato in Kenwood bowl. Add kelp, vegetable salt, pepper and cheese and mix until combined.

*To finish pie:* Roll half pastry out thinly and line a round 23 cm (9 inch) pie plate. Place filling into pie dish, shaping into a high dome shape in centre. Brush pastry rim with cold water. Roll remaining pastry out to a round and cover pie. Trim, seal, flake and scallop edge of pastry with sixteen scallops. Place pie plate on a baking tray and bake towards the top of a moderately hot oven at 190°C (375°F) for 30 minutes or until pastry is cooked. Serve hot with grilled or baked tomatoes.

**Note:** Kelp is a variety of dried seaweed which adds natural flavour to food. It may be bought in health food shops.

# Lentil Pie

*Serves 4.*

**250 g (1⅛ cups) lentils**
**1 onion, chopped**
**250 g (8 oz) mashed potato**
**1 tablespoon chopped parsley**
**1 tomato, peeled and chopped**
**salt and pepper**

Wash lentils in cold water, drain well. Place lentils and onion (chopped in a blender or food processor) in a pan with sufficient water to cover. Bring to the boil and boil gently until lentils are quite tender and soft. Drain well, then mix to a purée in a blender. Mix lentil and onion purée with remaining ingredients (previously prepared in the Kenwood mixer and blender) and add salt and pepper to taste. Place mixture neatly in a buttered pie dish and bake in a moderate oven at 180°C (350°F) for 20 minutes or until browned and crisp on top. Serve hot as an accompaniment to a curry or serve as a main course accompanied by mixed salads.

# Vegetable Protein Pies

*Makes 4.*

**250 g (1 quantity) wholemeal pastry (see page 13)**

*Filling:*
**60 g (2 tablespoons) margarine**
**1 large onion, chopped**
**1 tomato, chopped**
**½ green pepper, seeded and chopped**
**½ cup textured vegetable protein (TVP)**
**115 g can baked beans**
**3 tablespoons sultanas or raisins**
**1 teaspoon salt**
**beaten egg to glaze**

Prepare pastry according to recipe and chill well.

*Filling:* Heat margarine in a pan and gently fry onion (chopped in a blender or food processor) until soft and transparent, add tomato and green pepper (also prepared in a blender or food processor) and fry gently for a further 5 minutes, stirring occasionally. Stir in TVP, baked beans, sultanas and salt and remove from heat. Cool.

*To finish pies:* Roll pastry out thinly on a lightly floured board and cut out four 12 cm (5 inch) circles and line four 8 cm (3 inch) individual pie tins. Cut out four 8 cm (3 inch) circles for the tops of the pies. Divide cold filling between the pie cases. Brush edge of pie cases with cold water, place pastry tops over and seal edges, then flake and scallop edges neatly with a round-bladed knife. Make a neat hole in top of each pie with a skewer. Brush tops of pies with beaten egg. Place pies on a baking tray and bake towards the top of a hot oven at 200°C (400°F) for 20 minutes or until cooked. Cool on a wire cooling tray. Serve pies warm or cold with mixed salads or serve for a picnic or packed lunch.

**Note:** TVP or textured vegetable protein is made from nourishing soya beans, which are rich in protein. It is sold in health food shops.

# Ratatouille Pie

*Serves 4-6.*

**185 g (1 quantity) pâte brisée (see page 12)**

*Filling:*
**250 g (8 oz) eggplant**
**1 onion, finely chopped**
**2 tomatoes, chopped**
**1 small green or red pepper, seeded and chopped**
**2 small zucchini, sliced**
**2 tablespoons olive oil**
**60 g (2 tablespoons) butter**
**1 x 60 g egg**
**3 tablespoons cream**
**2 tablespoons grated Parmesan cheese**
**1 teaspoon salt**
**¼ teaspoon white pepper**
**beaten egg to glaze**

Prepare pâte brisée according to recipe and chill well.

*Filling:* Trim eggplant and cut into 1 cm (½ inch) cubes. Sprinkle with salt and leave to drain for 30 minutes. Meanwhile, chop onion, tomatoes and green or red pepper in either a blender or a food processor and slice zucchini (in a food processor). Heat oil in a large frying pan and fry eggplant for 3 minutes or until soft. Heat butter in a frying pan and fry onion until soft and golden, add tomatoes, pepper and zucchini, cover and simmer over a low heat for 10 minutes. Beat egg, cream, Parmesan cheese, salt and pepper all together in an electric mixer or food processor.

*To finish pie:* Transfer eggplant with a slotted spoon to a 1 litre (4 cup) pie dish. Spread onion mixture on top and pour egg mixture over. Roll pastry out to an oval and cover pie as for Steak and Kidney Pie (see page 22). Glaze pastry with beaten egg. Place pie dish on a baking tray and bake towards the top of a hot oven at 220°C (425°F) for 25-30 minutes until pastry is golden and cooked. Serve hot, with slices of ham or corned beef if liked.

# Russian Cabbage Pie

*Serves 6-8.*

**375 g (1½ quantities) puff, rough puff or flaky pastry (see pages 15, 16)**

**Filling:**
**¼ cabbage, finely shredded**
**1 onion, finely chopped**
**90 g (3 tablespoons) butter**
**3 hard-boiled eggs, chopped**
**60 g (½ cup) cheese, grated**
**60 ml (¼ cup) sour cream**
**1 teaspoon dried dill**
**salt and pepper**
**beaten egg to glaze**

Prepare pastry according to recipe and chill well.

*Filling:* Gently fry cabbage and onion (both prepared in a food processor) in butter in a large, heavy frying pan for 5 minutes, stirring frequently. Remove from heat, stir in eggs, cheese (both prepared in a food processor), sour cream and dill and season to taste with salt and pepper.

*To finish pie:* Divide pastry in half, roll half out to a round and line a 23 cm (9 inch) round pie plate. Place cabbage mixture in pie dish. Roll out remaining pastry to a round large enough for the top of the pie. Brush rim of pastry with cold water, place round of pastry on top, press edges to seal, then trim neatly. Flake and flute (or scallop) edge, then decorate top of pie with leaves made from pastry trimmings. Brush top of pie with beaten egg. Place pie dish on a baking tray and bake towards the top of a hot oven at 200°C (400°F) for 30-40 minutes, until puffed and golden. Serve pie hot in thick wedges with a stroganoff or similar beef casserole, in place of potatoes or rice.

# Silverbeet and Rice Pie

*Serves 6-8.*

**250 g (1 quantity) puff, rough puff or flaky pastry (see pages 15, 16)**

**Filling:**
**⅓ cup olive oil**
**2 onions, finely chopped**
**2 stalks celery, finely chopped**
**1 cup cooked rice ( ⅓ cup raw)**

**250 g (approx. 2½ cups) spinach, washed, dried and chopped**
**¼ cup chopped fresh basil**
**3 cloves garlic, crushed**
**beaten egg to glaze**

Make pastry according to recipe and chill in refrigerator until required.

*Filling:* In a large heavy-based frying pan, heat olive oil and gently fry onion and celery (both chopped in a blender or food processor) until tender and lightly coloured. Add rice, spinach, basil (both chopped in a blender or food processor) and garlic and cook over a medium heat for 5-10 minutes. Remove from heat and allow to cool.

*To finish pie:* Cut off one-third of the pastry and stand aside. On a lightly floured board, roll out the two-thirds of the pastry to a round and line a 23 cm (9 inch) pie plate. Prick the bottom, trim edge of pastry and spoon in the filling. Roll out remaining pastry large enough to cover pie. Brush rim of pastry (on pie dish) with cold water and place cover on top. Seal, trim, flake and flute (or scallop) edges with sixteen scallops. Brush top of pastry (not flaked edges) with beaten egg. Make a steam hole in centre of pie. Stand pie plate on a baking tray and bake towards the top of a hot oven at 200°C (400°F) for 30 minutes, or until pastry is cooked and golden. Serve hot in wedges with a casserole as a substitute for potatoes or serve as a vegetarian meal accompanied by baked tomatoes.

# Soya Bean Pasties

*Makes 6.*

**250 g (1 quantity) short crust pastry (see page 11)**

*Filling:*
**½ cup mashed soya loaf**
**125 g (½ cup) fresh breadcrumbs**
**1 small onion, finely chopped**
**½ cup cashew nuts, finely chopped**
**1 tablespoon chopped parsley**
**1 x 60 g egg**
**60 ml (¼ cup) milk**
**salt and pepper**
**beaten egg to glaze**

Prepare pastry according to recipe and chill well.

*Filling:* The first five ingredients may be prepared in a blender or food processor. Mix all ingredients together in either a blender or food processor.

*To finish pasties:* Roll pastry out thinly and cut out six rounds by cutting around a saucer. Turn rounds over and place 2-3 tablespoons of filling in centre of each. Brush edges of rounds with cold water then press together firmly to seal and roll edge, as for Cornish Pasties (see page 21). Place pasties on a greased baking tray and brush with beaten egg. Bake at the top of a hot oven at 220°C (425°F) for 20 minutes or until golden brown and cooked. Cool on a wire cooling tray until firm before serving.

Serve hot with home-made tomato sauce and vegetables or cold with salad. Good for a packed lunch or picnic.

# Spanakopita

**(Cheese and Spinach Pie)**

*Serves 12 as a first course.*

**16 sheets (approx. 2 packets) phyllo pastry**
**185 g (¾ cup) butter, melted**

*Filling:*
**3 tablespoons olive oil**
**1 medium onion, finely chopped**
**6 shallots, finely chopped**
**1 kg (2 lb) spinach or 2 packets frozen spinach *or* 2 cans spinach**
**4 x 60 g eggs**
**250 g (8 oz) feta cheese, crumbled**
**¼ cup chopped parsley**
**¼ cup chopped fresh dill or 2 teaspoons dried dill**
**1 teaspoon salt**
**freshly ground black pepper**

Keep phyllo pastry sealed until required.

*Filling:* Heat oil in a heavy frying pan and gently fry onion and shallots (both prepared in a blender or food processor) until soft and golden, about 5 minutes. Wash spinach, drain well and shred finely, using the Kenwood shredder attachment or food processor. If using frozen spinach, allow to thaw then drain well. If using canned spinach, drain well. Add spinach to pan, cover and simmer for 5 minutes. Add parsley and dill (chopped in a blender or food processor). Beat eggs in an electric mixer, add feta cheese, salt and pepper and mix well, then add spinach mixture and mix until evenly combined.

*To finish pie:* Brush bottom and sides of a lamington tin with melted butter. Unwrap one packet of phyllo pastry and unfold the sheets of pastry carefully. Place a sheet of phyllo pastry in the lamington tin and brush with melted butter. Repeat layering eight sheets of phyllo pastry into the tin, brushing top of each layer with melted butter. Keep phyllo pastry covered with a clean, cold, damp tea towel while not working with it to prevent it from turning dry and brittle. Spread spinach mixture evenly over pastry. Open second packet of phyllo pastry and cover spinach with eight more sheets of pastry, brushing each with melted butter. Brush top layer with melted butter. Trim edges of pie with kitchen scissors and fold edges in neatly. Mark top of pie diagonally into diamonds. Bake in a moderate oven at 180°C (350°F) for 30-40 minutes, until top of pie is crisp, puffy and golden. Serve hot or warm as a first course or serve in small pieces, accompanied by olives, with pre-dinner drinks. This is also an ideal dish to serve at a buffet party.

Onion Tart Niçoise, Ham and Pineapple Quiche and Seafood Flan
*(see pages 52, 51, 53)*

# SAVOURY FLANS AND TARTS

The most famous savoury flan or tart is Quiche Lorraine, the open savoury tart filled with eggs, cream and bacon which is made in the province of Lorraine in the north-east of France. A slice of hot savoury flan or tart may be served as a first course when entertaining, and it is an ideal dish to serve for lunch or for a light supper when accompanied by a tossed salad and a chilled light white wine. Some flans are equally tempting served cold and can be taken on a picnic or served in a packed lunch.

The crust which holds the filling of a savoury flan or tart should be thin and crisp. Pâte brisée is the ideal pastry to use for a quiche and it tastes delicious. Your Kenwood mixer or food processor makes it beautifully.

# Tips

To line a flan tin, lift the pastry over a rolling pin and unroll into the tin, then, working from the centre, press all the air out from underneath with the back of your fingers, and finally roll over the top of the flan tin lightly with the rolling pin to trim off the edges.

Baking beans may be kept in a storage jar in a cool dry place and used for baking 'blind' for up to a year before they turn rancid.

To remove a flan from a flan tin, carefully stand the tin on top of a large flat-topped jar and gently remove the side of the flan tin. Transfer the flan and the tin base to a cooling tray or serving plate, then carefully loosen flan with a palette knife and remove the base.

Pizza Pie
(see page 56)

# Egg and Salmon Tart

Serves 4-6.

**185 g (1 quantity) pâte brisée or sour cream pastry (see pages 12, 13)**

*Filling:*
**250 g can salmon, drained**
**2 teaspoons lemon juice**
**1 onion, finely chopped**
**1 tomato, chopped**
**6 x 60 g eggs**
**salt and pepper**
**60 g (¼ cup) Cheddar cheese, grated**
**½ cup crushed savoury biscuits**

Make pastry according to recipe and line a deep 20 cm (8 inch) flan tin.

*Filling:* Lightly flake salmon with a fork and remove any bones. Stir lemon juice and onion (chopped in a blender or food processor) into salmon.

*To finish tart:* Place salmon mixture in prepared pastry case and sprinkle tomato over. Carefully break eggs on top. Sprinkle salt and pepper, grated cheese and biscuit crumbs over. Bake in the centre of a hot oven at 200°C (400°F) for 10 minutes, then reduce temperature to moderate, 180°C (350°F), for a further 20-30 minutes or until eggs are cooked and cheese and crumbs are golden. Serve hot with a tossed salad.

# Cheese and Leek Flan

*Serves 4-6.*

**185 g (1 quantity) pâte brisée or
  (¾ quantity) cheese pastry (see pages
  12, 13)**

*Filling:*
**60 g (2 tablespoons) butter
2 large leeks, well washed and sliced
125 ml (½ cup) water
2 x 60 g eggs
125 ml (½ cup) cream
½ teaspoon salt
pinch of white pepper
pinch of ground nutmeg
125 g (1 cup) Cheddar cheese, grated**

Make pastry according to recipe and line a
23 cm (9 inch) flan tin.

*Filling:* Heat butter in a frying pan and
gently fry leeks (sliced in a food processor), stirring occasionally, until golden
brown. Add water and simmer gently until
water evaporates, then leave to cool. Beat
eggs, cream, salt, pepper and nutmeg all
together. Stir cheese (grated in a food
processor) and leeks into egg mixture.

*To finish flan:* Pour filling into prepared
pastry case and bake towards the top of
a hot oven at 200°C (400°F) for 10 minutes,
then reduce to moderately slow, 160°C
(325°F), for a further 20 minutes. Serve hot
with a tossed salad.

# Corn and Cheese Flan

*Serves 4-6.*

**185 g (¾ quantity) short crust or cheese
  pastry (see pages 11, 13)
30 g (½ cup) all-bran, crushed**

*Filling:*
**300 g can sweet corn niblets
3 x 60 g eggs
250 ml (1 cup) milk
½ teaspoon salt
¼ teaspoon white pepper
125 g (4 oz) mozzarella cheese, thinly
  sliced**

Make pastry according to recipe, adding
the crushed all-bran to the flour and salt.
Roll pastry out and line a 23 cm (9 inch)
flan tin.

*Filling:* Drain sweet corn. Beat eggs with
milk, salt and pepper.

*To finish flan:* Sprinkle sweet corn over
base of pastry case, pour egg mixture over
and top with slices of mozzarella cheese.
Bake towards the top of a hot oven at
200°C (400°F) for 35 minutes or until
golden brown and set. Serve hot while
puffed, accompanied by a tossed salad.

# Crab Tart

*Serves 4-6.*

**185 g (1 quantity) pâte brisée, or
  (¾ quantity) short crust pastry (see
  pages 11, 12)**

*Filling:*
**250 g can crab
1 tablespoon chopped shallots
1 tablespoon chopped parsley
2 tablespoons lemon juice
2 x 60 g eggs
125 ml (½ cup) cream
125 ml (½ cup) milk
salt
white pepper**

Make pastry according to recipe and chill
well.

*Filling:* Drain crabmeat, flake with a fork
and remove any bony tissue. Mix crabmeat
with shallots and parsley (both chopped in
a blender or food processor) and lemon
juice. Beat eggs and stir in cream and milk.
Season to taste with salt and pepper.

*To finish tart:* Roll pastry out and line a
23 cm (9 inch) flan tin. Prick bottom of
pastry case, line with a piece of greaseproof paper and a layer of dried beans.
Bake 'blind' towards the top of a hot oven
at 220°C (425°F) for 10 minutes then
remove from oven and remove 'blind' filling,
(paper and beans). Place crabmeat mixture
in pastry case and pour egg mixture over.
Reduce oven temperature to moderately
hot, at 190°C (375°F) and bake for 20-30
minutes or until filling is set and golden.
Serve hot accompanied by a chilled dry
white wine and a tossed salad.

# Crayfish and Asparagus Flan

*Serves 4-6.*

**185 g (1 quantity) pâte brisée or
(¾ quantity) short crust pastry (see
pages 11, 12)**

**Filling:**
**250 g (8 oz) asparagus, fresh or canned**
**125 g (4 oz) cooked crayfish**
**2 x 60 g eggs**
**125 ml (½ cup) cream**
**125 ml (½ cup) milk**
**salt and pepper**
**2 tablespoons grated Parmesan cheese**

Make pastry according to directions in
recipe and chill well. Line a 23 cm (9 inch)
flan tin with the pastry and prick base well
with a fork.

*Filling:* Cook asparagus if fresh, drain well,
cut into 2.5 cm (1 inch) lengths. Drain
canned asparagus and cut into short
pieces. Flake crayfish. Beat eggs with
cream, milk and salt and pepper to taste.

*To finish flan:* Place crayfish and asparagus in pastry case, pour egg mixture over
and sprinkle with Parmesan cheese. Bake
towards the top of a hot oven at 200°C
(425°F) for 20-25 minutes or until set and
well browned. Serve hot accompanied by a
chilled dry white wine and a tossed salad.

# Ham and Pineapple Quiche

*Serves 6.*

**8 sheets phyllo pastry**
**90 g (3 tablespoons) butter, melted**

**Filling:**
**125 g (4 oz) cooked ham, chopped**
**1 tablespoon chopped fresh mint**
**3 x 60 g eggs**
**250 ml (1 cup) evaporated milk**
**1 teaspoon salt**
**freshly ground black pepper**
**½ teaspoon mustard powder**
**450 g can pineapple pieces, drained**
**1 tablespoon grated Parmesan cheese**
**sprigs of mint for garnish**

Line a 23 cm (9 inch) flan tin or pie dish
with 8 sheets of phyllo pastry, brushing
each layer with melted butter. Trim edges
neatly with kitchen scissors.

*Filling:* Chop ham and mint in a blender or
food processor. Beat eggs, evaporated
milk and seasonings all together in a
mixing bowl.

*To finish quiche:* Sprinkle chopped ham
and mint over pastry case, then top with
drained pineapple pieces. Carefully spoon
egg mixture over and sprinkle Parmesan
cheese over the top. Bake towards the top
of a moderate oven at 180°C (350°F) for
30 minutes or until set. Serve hot,
garnished with mint sprigs, accompanied
by a tossed salad and a chilled rosé wine.

# Swedish Fish Tart

*Serves 4-6.*

**250 g (1 quantity) short crust pastry (see
page 11)**

**Filling:**
**250 g (8 oz) smoked haddock**
**125 ml (½ cup) milk**
**2 x 60 g eggs**
**300 ml (1 carton/jar) sour cream**
**2 hard-boiled eggs, chopped**
**2 tablespoons chopped parsley**
**½ teaspoon salt**
**¼ teaspoon pepper**
**¼ teaspoon ground nutmeg**

Make pastry according to recipe and chill
well.

*Filling:* Poach haddock in milk for 10
minutes until tender. Remove skin and any
bones and flake fish with a fork. Beat eggs
and stir in haddock, milk, sour cream,
hard-boiled eggs and parsley (both prepared in a blender or food processor) and
seasonings.

*To finish tart:* Roll pastry out and line a
deep 20 cm (8 inch) flan tin. Stand flan tin
on a baking tray and carefully spoon filling
into prepared pastry case. Bake towards
the top of a moderately hot oven at 190°C
(375°F) for 10 minutes, then reduce temperature to moderate, 180°C (350°F), and
continue baking for a further 20 minutes
or until set. Serve hot with a tossed salad.

# Mushroom Tart

*Serves 4-6.*

**185 g (1 quantity) pâte brisée or**
**(¾ quantity) short crust pastry (see**
**pages 11, 12)**

*Filling:*
**250 g (8 oz) mushrooms, thinly sliced**
**1 onion, finely chopped**
**30 g (1 tablespoon) butter or margarine**
**1 tablespoon plain flour**
**125 ml (½ cup) milk**
**125 ml (½ cup) cream**
**2 egg yolks**
**salt and pepper**
**pinch of ground nutmeg**
**60 g (¼ cup) Gruyère or Parmesan**
**cheese, grated**
**6 mushroom caps, fried in butter for**
**garnish**

Make pastry according to recipe and chill well.

*Filling:* Prepare mushrooms and onions in a food processor. Sauté mushrooms and onion in butter in a covered pan until soft. Add flour and stir the roux over a medium heat for 1 minute. Add milk and bring to the boil, stirring continuously. Stir in cream, egg yolks, salt, pepper and nutmeg.

*To finish tart:* Roll pastry out and line a 23 cm (9 inch) flan tin. Prick bottom of case, line with greaseproof paper and dried beans. Bake 'blind' towards the top of a hot oven at 220°C (425°F) for 10 minutes, then remove from oven and remove paper and beans. Pour filling into pastry case and sprinkle with cheese. Reduce oven temperature to moderately hot, 190°C (375°F), and bake for 15-20 minutes or until filling is set. Serve hot topped with fried mushrooms.

# Quiche Lorraine

*Serves 4-6.*

**185 g (1 quantity) pâte brisée (see page**
**12)**

*Filling:*
**6 rashers lean bacon**
**1 teaspoon butter**
**2 x 60 g eggs**
**2 egg yolks**
**250 ml (1 cup) cream**

**½ teaspoon salt**
**¼ teaspoon white pepper**
**125 g (½ cup) Swiss cheese, grated**
**parsley sprig for garnish**

Make pastry according to recipe and chill well.

*Filling:* Cut rind and any bones off bacon and cut into 5 mm (¼ inch) dice or chop in a blender or food processor. Heat butter in a frying pan and fry bacon until crisp and golden brown; do not overcook. Transfer from pan with a slotted spoon and drain on kitchen paper towels. Beat eggs, egg yolks, cream, salt and pepper together. Stir in grated cheese.

*To finish quiche:* Roll pastry out and line a 23 cm (9 inch) flan tin. Prick bottom of pastry flan with fork, place on a baking tray and bake 'blind' in a hot oven at 220°C (425°F) for 10 minutes, remove baking beans and paper ('blind' filling) and bake for a further 5 minutes. Remove from oven, sprinkle bacon over bottom of pastry case and spoon egg mixture into it. Bake in a moderately hot oven at 190°C (375°F) for 25-30 minutes until custard is puffed and golden brown. Serve immediately accompanied by a tossed salad.

# Onion Tart Niçoise

*Serves 4-6.*

**185 g (1 quantity) pâte brisée (see page**
**12)**

*Filling:*
**750 g (1½ lb) brown onions**
**125 ml (½ cup) olive oil**
**1 teaspoon salt**
**freshly ground black pepper**
**1 large tomato**
**1 tablespoon chopped fresh oregano *or***
**1 teaspoon dried oregano**
**4-6 pitted ripe olives, sliced**
**2 teaspoons chopped parsley**

Make pastry according to instructions and chill well.

*Filling:* Peel 500 g (1 lb) onions and slice thinly. In a large heavy-based frying pan, heat olive oil and add sliced onions, salt and pepper. Cover and fry gently over a medium heat for 30-40 minutes, or until lightly coloured and very limp. Drain onions in a sieve over a bowl, reserving oil, and allow to cool. Slice all but 1 small onion of the remaining onions into 5 mm (¼ inch) thick slices. Carefully slice tomato the same thickness. Slice the remaining small onion also in 5 mm (¼ inch) slices and place to one side.

*To finish tart:* On a lightly floured surface, roll pastry out to a round 3 mm (⅛ inch) thick and line a 23 cm (9 inch) flan tin. Prick base of pastry case and place flan tin on a baking tray. Spread fried onions in pastry case. Arrange overlapping slices of onion around edge of flan, then arrange overlapping slices of tomato inside row of onion. Arrange slices of small onion in centre. Brush onion and tomato slices generously with reserved oil and sprinkle with oregano and more salt and pepper to taste. Bake tart towards the top of a hot oven at 220°C (425°F) for 40-45 minutes, basting with more oil if onions and tomato look dry. Cool slightly and arrange sliced olives on the outer ring of onion slices and sprinkle tomato with chopped parsley. Serve immediately accompanied by a tossed salad.

# Seafood Flan

*Serves 4-6.*

**250 g (1 quantity) rich short crust pastry, minus sugar (see page 12)**

*Filling:*
**500 g (1 lb) prawns**
**250 g (8 oz) white fish fillet, bream or jewfish**
**125 ml (½ cup) water**
**3 x 60 g eggs**
**125 ml (½ cup) cream**
**squeeze of lemon juice**
**3 teaspoons finely chopped parsley**
**1 teaspoon salt**
**¼ teaspoon white pepper**
**pinch of cayenne pepper**
**freshly grated nutmeg for garnish**

Prepare pastry according to recipe and chill well.

*Filling:* Reserve a few prawns for garnish and shell and devein remaining prawns. Place fish fillet on a heatproof plate, pour water over, cover and steam over a pan of boiling water for 15 minutes or until cooked. Flake fish and reserve ¼ cup fish stock. Beat eggs, cream and fish stock together and add prawns, fish, lemon juice, parsley and seasonings.

*To finish flan:* Roll pastry out on a lightly floured board to a round and line a deep 20 cm (8 inch) or shallow 23 cm (9 inch) flan tin. Prick bottom of flan and bake 'blind' (lined with greaseproof paper and filled with a layer of dried beans) in the middle of a hot oven at 200°C (400°F) for 15 minutes. Remove paper and beans, pour filling into flan case and grate nutmeg over the top. Bake for a further 45 minutes for a deep flan, 25-30 minutes for a shallow flan. Serve immediately while puffed and golden, accompanied by a dry white wine and followed by a tossed salad.

# Tomato Flan

*Serves 4-6.*

**185 g (1 quantity) low cholesterol whole-meal or cheese pastry (see pages 13, 14)**

*Filling:*
**30 g (1 tablespoon) butter or margarine**
**1 onion, finely chopped**
**2 cloves garlic, crushed**
**5 large tomatoes, peeled, seeded and chopped**
**1 tablespoon tomato paste**
**3 tablespoons grated Parmesan cheese**
**¼ teaspoon dried basil**
**salt and pepper**
**1 tablespoon sliced black olives and Parmesan cheese for garnish**

Prepare pastry according to recipe and chill well.

*Filling:* Heat butter in a saucepan and gently fry onion and garlic until soft and golden. Add chopped tomato, tomato paste, Parmesan cheese, basil, salt and pepper and simmer for 10 minutes, stirring frequently.

*To finish flan:* Roll pastry out on a lightly floured board to a round and line a 23 cm (9 inch) flan tin placed on a baking tray. Prick base and bake 'blind' in a moderately hot oven at 190°C (375°F) for 15 minutes. Remove 'blind' filling (greaseproof paper and beans) and bake for a further 5 minutes. Remove flan case from oven, pour filling in and spread it level. Sprinkle sliced black olives and 1 tablespoon Parmesan cheese over filling and return flan to oven for a further 15 minutes or until filling is firm and pastry is cooked. Serve flan immediately, straight from the oven, accompanied by a tossed green salad.

# Spinach Flan

*Serves 4-6.*

185 g (1 quantity) wholemeal wheatgerm
    pastry (see page 14)

*Filling:*
500 g (1 lb) spinach or silverbeet
2 rashers bacon
1 onion, finely chopped
1 clove garlic, crushed
30 g (1 tablespoon) butter or margarine
2 x 60 g eggs
125 g (½ cup) cottage cheese
3 tablespoons cream
pinch of ground nutmeg
salt and pepper
2 tablespoons grated Parmesan cheese for
    sprinkling

Make pastry according to recipe and chill
well.

*Filling:* Wash and trim spinach and shred
in either a Kenwood slicer and shredder
attachment or a food processor. Cook
spinach in the water clinging to the leaves
in a covered pan for 5 minutes, drain well.
Mix spinach to a purée in a blender. Rind
bacon and remove bones. Chop bacon and
onion in a blender or food processor. Fry
bacon, onion and garlic in butter until
onion is soft and golden. Beat eggs,
cottage cheese, cream, nutmeg, salt and
pepper together in a bowl or a food processor. Add spinach and bacon mixture
and mix together.

*To finish flan:* Roll pastry out to a round
and line a 23 cm (9 inch) flan tin. Bake
'blind' at the top of a hot oven at 220°C
(425°F) for 10 minutes. Remove 'blind'
filling (beans and greaseproof paper),
spread spinach filling in pastry case and
sprinkle with Parmesan cheese. Bake in a
hot oven at 200°C (400°F) for 20-30
minutes or until filling is set and cheese is
golden. Serve hot or warm with a mixed
salad.

# Swiss Cheese Tart

*Serves 4-6.*

185 g (1 quantity) pâte brisée or
    (¾ quantity) short crust pastry (see
    pages 11, 12)

*Filling:*
1½ tablespoons oil
1 onion, finely chopped
¼ teaspoon paprika
125 g (1 cup) Emmenthal cheese, grated
125 g (1 cup) Gruyère cheese, grated
2 x 60 g eggs
125 ml (½ cup) cream
125 ml (½ cup) milk
¼ teaspoon salt
⅛ teaspoon ground nutmeg

Prepare pastry according to recipe and
chill well.

*Filling:* Heat oil in a frying pan, add onion
(chopped in a blender or food processor)
and cook until soft and transparent. Stir in
paprika. Grate the two cheeses in a food
processor and mix together. Beat the eggs,
cream, milk, salt and nutmeg together in a
bowl.

*To finish tart:* Roll out pastry on a lightly
floured board to a round and line a 23 cm
(9 inch) flan tin. Place a piece of greaseproof paper in the pastry case and fill with
baking beans. Bake 'blind' towards the top
of a hot oven at 220°C (425°F) for 10
minutes. Remove greaseproof paper and
beans and bake for a further 10 minutes.
Cool before filling. Place flan tin on a
baking tray. Spread half the mixed cheeses
in the pastry case, cover with fried onions,
then place remaining cheese on top. Pour
egg mixture carefully over the cheese.
Bake in a moderate oven at 180°C (350°F)
for 10 minutes, then increase to hot at
220°C (425°F) and bake for a further 15
minutes or until golden brown and puffy.
Serve hot or warm accompanied by tomato
salad.

# PIZZA PIES

The original Italian pizza comes from Naples, but like many traditional dishes it has changed while travelling to all corners of the earth. A true pizza has a base made from a yeast dough which is light-textured when baked. It has a rich tomato sauce on top and may be varied by sprinkling with chopped ham, salami, mushrooms, prawns, anchovies, capers, olives and peppers. For a pizza which is quick and easy to make, a pastry dough or a scone dough may be used in place of the yeast dough. Pizzas are a good standby to have on hand in your freezer; it is a good idea to make a double quantity and eat one and freeze the other.

# Tip

Use the Kenwood dough hook for kneading your pizza yeast dough but remember it is very powerful so do not overmix.

# Pizza Meat Pie

*Serves 4-6.*

*Crust:*
**500 g (1 lb) finely minced topside beef**
**60 g (½ cup) dry breadcrumbs**
**60 g (½ cup) powdered milk**
**125 ml (½ cup) water**
**1 teaspoon salt**
**¼ teaspoon pepper**
**1 clove garlic, crushed**

*Topping:*
**150 g can tomato paste**
**125 g (1 cup) Cheddar cheese, grated**
**125 g (4 oz) button mushrooms**
**1 teaspoon dried oregano**
**2 tablespoons grated Parmesan cheese**
**sliced stuffed olives for garnish**

*Crust:* Mince beef with either the Kenwood mincer attachment or in a food processor. Mix minced beef, breadcrumbs, powdered milk, water, salt, pepper and garlic all together in an electric mixer or food processor.

*Topping:* Mix tomato paste with grated Cheddar cheese (grated in a food processor). Reserve half mushrooms for top, slice remainder (in a food processor) and add to tomato paste mixture along with oregano.

*To finish pizza:* Pat mince mixture over the base and up the side of a 23 cm (9 inch) pizza tray or round pie dish or tart plate. Spread topping over meat. Cover opposite quarters of the pizza meat pie with quarter circles of greaseproof paper or foil and sprinkle Parmesan cheese over the alternate quarters. Remove paper and decorate top with thickly sliced reserved button mushrooms and slices of stuffed olives. Bake in the middle of a moderate oven at 180°C (350°F) for 30-40 minutes until meat is cooked. Serve hot in segments with French or Italian bread and a tossed salad.

# Pizza Pie

*Serves 4 as a main meal; serves 24 as a party savoury.*

**400 g (1 quantity) pizza dough (see page 16)**

*Sauce:*
**3 tablespoons oil**
**2 onions, finely chopped**
**3 cloves garlic, crushed**
**2 x 450 g cans tomatoes**
**185 g can tomato paste**
**3 teaspoons dried oregano**
**3 teaspoons chopped fresh basil *or***
 **2 teaspoons dried basil**
**1 bay leaf**
**2 teaspoons sugar**
**3 teaspoons salt**
**freshly ground black pepper**

*Topping:*
**extra olive oil for cooking**
**250 g (8 oz) mozzarella cheese**
**30 g (¼ cup) finely grated Parmesan cheese**

Prepare pizza dough according to recipe.

*Sauce:* Heat oil in a heavy-based pan and gently fry chopped onion (prepared in a blender or food processor) for 7-8 minutes, stirring frequently until soft and transparent but not browned. Add garlic and fry gently for 1-2 minutes. Stir in coarsely chopped tomatoes and their liquor, and the remaining sauce ingredients. Cover and bring to the boil, then reduce heat and simmer for 1 hour, stirring occasionally. Remove bay leaf and season to taste if necessary. The sauce should be thick and smooth. If too thin, simmer a little longer, uncovered, to reduce the liquid. Allow sauce to cool, then purée in blender at maximum speed for 20 seconds.

*To finish pizza:* Divide dough into two, knead and shape each half into a small round and pat into a circle using the palm of the hand. Finally, roll circles out thinly with a rolling pin and press into two 30 cm (12 inch) greased pizza pans.

*Topping:* Brush edges of pizza dough with olive oil and cover each with 1 cup sauce. Sprinkle mozzarella and Parmesan cheeses over sauce and drizzle 2 tablespoons olive oil over each pizza. Bake, one at a time, at the top of a hot oven at 220°C (425°F) for 18-20 minutes until crust is golden and cooked. Cut pizzas into wedges and serve warm, accompanied by rosé wine and a tossed salad.

# Scone Dough Pizza

*Serves 4 as a main meal; serves 6-8 as a snack.*

**250 g (1 quantity) scone dough (see page 17)**

*Topping:*
**30 g (1 tablespoon) butter or margarine**
**1 onion, finely chopped**
**2 tomatoes, coarsely chopped**
**250 g (2 cups) Cheddar cheese, grated**
**1 can anchovy fillets, drained**
**4 black olives, halved, optional**

Prepare scone dough according to recipe.

*Topping:* Heat butter in a heavy-based frying pan and gently fry onion (chopped in a blender or food processor) for 5-6 minutes or until soft and transparent. Add tomato and continue to fry gently for a further 4-5 minutes or until mixture is pulpy.

*To finish pizza:* Roll scone dough out to a 25 cm (10 inch) diameter round, 1 cm (½ inch) thick. Place dough on a lightly greased baking tray or pizza pan. Spread topping on top of prepared dough and cover with grated cheese (prepared in a food processor). Arrange anchovy fillets and olives decoratively on top. Bake towards the top of a hot oven at 200°C (400°F) for 15-20 minutes or until cooked. Serve immediately.

Healthy Apple Pie, Peach Pie and Steak and Kidney Pie
*(see pages 72, 76, 22)*

# Fish Pizza

*Serves 4 for a main meal; serves 8 as a snack or party savoury.*

**375 g (double quantity) short crust pastry (see page 11)**

*Topping:*
**500 g (1 lb) small white fish fillets, perch or redfish**
**2 tablespoons olive oil**
**½ teaspoon salt**
**extra olive oil**
**plain flour for sprinkling**
**8 fresh sage leaves**
**8 anchovy fillets**
**30 g (1 tablespoon) butter or margarine**

Prepare pastry according to recipe and chill well.

*Topping:* Skin fish, remove bones and cut fillets in pieces 5 cm (2 inches) long. Gently mix fish with olive oil and salt in a mixing bowl.

*To finish pizza:* Roll pastry out to a thin circle and line a 30 cm (12 inch) pizza tray. Brush dough lightly with olive oil and sprinkle with flour. Arrange pieces of fish, in two or three circles, on the pizza base, covering completely. Place sage leaves on top around edge and top these with anchovy fillets. Top with thin slices of butter. Bake at the top of a hot oven at 220°C (425°F) for 15-20 minutes or until cooked. Serve hot with a tossed salad and dry white wine.

**Note:** This pizza is ideal for using a fisherman's catch of very small fish.

# Wholemeal Vegetable Pizza

*Serves 4 for a main meal; serves 8 as a snack.*

**250 g (1 quantity) wholemeal wheatgerm pastry (see page 14)**

*Topping:*
**500 g (1 lb) zucchini**
**2 onions, thinly sliced**
**2 tomatoes, thinly sliced**

*Sauce:*
**250 ml (1 cup) milk**
**30 g (1 tablespoon) butter or margarine**
**2 tablespoons wholemeal flour**
**125 g (1 cup) Cheddar cheese, grated**
**salt and pepper**

Make pastry according to recipe and chill well.

*Topping:* Wash zucchini in cold water, top and tail, then slice thinly in a food processor. Prepare onions and tomatoes also in a food processor.

*Sauce:* Place milk, butter and flour in given order in a blender and mix until evenly combined. Pour mixture into a saucepan and bring to the boil, stirring continuously. Stir in cheese until melted and season to taste with salt and pepper.

*To finish pizza:* Roll pastry out on a lightly floured board to a thin round, place on a pizza tray and press to the edge of the tray. Arrange sliced zucchini in a layer on top of pastry, then cover with onions and tomatoes. Spread sauce over vegetables. Bake at the top of a hot oven at 200°C (400°F) for 25-30 minutes until pastry is cooked. Serve hot, cut in segments, accompanied by a tossed salad.

Mushroom and Tomato Tarts, Cheese Tricorns and Beef and Cabbage Piragi
*(see pages 66, 65 64)*

# POTATO TOPPED PIES

A tasty pie topped with creamy mashed potatoes is one of the most delicious budget saving dishes I know of.
Potatoes started to appear in recipes towards the end of the sixteenth century. A Gipsy Pie was a stodgy pie filled with potatoes, onion and butter and covered with pastry. Ten to One Pie was an old English north country favourite in which ten slices of potato were used to one slice of mutton as a pie filling. Thanks to the good rural sense of the country housewife, the potato eventually came out of the pie filling and was used as a topping in place of pastry in a shepherd's pie or cottage pie.
Most potato-topped pies have been invented to use up leftovers in a tasty dish. Some fresh flavouring ingredients and herbs and spices are added, along with the tricks of quick rechauffé cooking and the result is another mouth-watering savoury pie.

# Tips

Potato-topped pies are good tasty budget savers.

The Kenwood potato peeler attachment takes all the messy hard work out of peeling potatoes.

Use the K beater for mashing and creaming potatoes.

Use the Kenwood mincer attachment or food processor for mincing fresh or cooked meat.

# Potato Lattice Pie

*Serves 4-6.*

*Topping:*
**1 kg (2 lb) potatoes**
**60 g (2 tablespoons) butter or margarine**
**4 tablespoons 'top of milk' or cream**
**salt and white pepper**

*Filling:*
**125 g (4 oz) mushrooms, buttons or caps**
**60 g (2 tablespoons) butter or margarine**
**4 hard-boiled eggs**

*Cheese sauce:*
**30 g (1 tablespoon) butter or soft margarine**
**2 tablespoons plain flour**
**300 ml (approx. 1¼ cups) milk**
**60 g (½ cup) Cheddar cheese, grated**
**salt and pepper**

*Topping:* Peel potatoes in Kenwood potato peeler attachment and cook in a pan of boiling, salted water until tender. Drain potatoes well, return to pan and dry off over the heat, then remove from heat and mash with the Kenwood mixer until very smooth. Potatoes may also be mixed in a food processor until very smooth. Add butter, 'top of milk' and salt and pepper to taste and beat well until creamy.

*Filling:* Fry mushrooms in butter and quarter hard-boiled eggs.

*Cheese sauce:* Place all ingredients in a saucepan and whisk continuously with a balloon-shaped whisk over a medium heat until sauce boils and thickens, then simmer for 2 minutes.

*To finish pie:* Place half creamed potatoes in a layer over the bottom of an ovenproof serving dish or casserole. Place fried mushrooms and hard-boiled eggs on top of creamed potato and pour cheese sauce over. Place remaining creamed potato in a piping bag with a 1 cm (½ inch) star pipe and pipe a lattice design on top of sauce and rosettes around the edge of the dish. Brown pie under a hot grill or in a moderately hot oven at 190°C (375°F) for 20-30 minutes. Serve piping hot for supper.

# Curried Meat Pie

*Serves 4.*

**Filling:**
**375 g (3 cups) chopped cooked meat**
**1 tablespoon oil**
**1 onion, chopped**
**1 apple, peeled, cored and chopped**
**1 tablespoon curry powder**
**1 tablespoon plain flour**
**125 ml (½ cup) stock**
**2 tablespoons sultanas**
**1 tablespoon chutney**
**1 tomato, chopped**
**salt and pepper**

**Topping:**
**750 g (1½ lb) potatoes**
**60 g (2 tablespoons) butter or margarine**
**2 tablespoons milk**

*Filling:* Mince meat in the Kenwood mincer attachment or in a food processor. Heat oil in a heavy-based pan and gently fry onion and apple (prepared in either a blender or a food processor) for 5 minutes. Add curry powder and flour and stir over heat for 1-2 minutes. Add stock and bring to the boil, stirring continuously. Remove from heat and stir in minced meat, sultanas, chutney and tomato (chopped in a food processor). Season to taste with salt and pepper.

*Topping:* Peel potatoes in a Kenwood potato peeler attachment then cook in boiling salted water until tender. Drain potatoes, place in Kenwood bowl and beat with a K beater at minimum speed for 10 seconds, add butter and milk and mix at speed 5 until creamy and smooth.

*To finish pie:* Place filling in a pie dish. Spread creamed potato over filling, spread smooth with a round-bladed knife, then fork attractively with the tines of a fork. Heat pie in a hot oven at 200°C (400°F) for 20-30 minutes or until pie is browned and bubbling hot. Serve hot with a green vegetable.

# Lamb and Zucchini Pie

*Serves 4-6.*

**Filling:**
**375 g (3 cups) chopped, cooked lamb**
**3 onions, finely chopped**
**2 cloves garlic, crushed**
**90 g (3 tablespoons) butter or margarine**
**6 medium zucchini, sliced**
**2 large tomatoes, skinned and chopped**
**125 ml (½ cup) lamb gravy or beef stock**
**salt and pepper**

**Topping:**
**1 kg (2 lb) potatoes**
**45 g (1½ tablespoons) butter or margarine**
**1 tablespoon milk**

*Filling:* Trim lamb and mince in the Kenwood mincer attachment or in a food processor. Chop onion in a blender or food processor, then gently fry onion and garlic in butter, in a heavy-based frying pan for 5 minutes or until onion is soft and transparent. Add zucchini (sliced in a food processor) to pan and gently fry, stirring occasionally, for 10 minutes. Stir in lamb, tomatoes (chopped in a blender or food processor) and gravy and season to taste with salt and pepper. Bring to the boil, then simmer for 15 minutes.

*Topping:* Peel potatoes in a Kenwood potato peeler attachment then boil in salted water until tender. Drain potatoes, place in Kenwood bowl and beat with a K beater on minimum speed for 10 seconds, add butter and milk, turn to speed 5 for 20 seconds or until creamy and smooth.

*To finish pie:* Place lamb and zucchini mixture in a pie dish. Pipe rosettes of creamed potato over the lamb mixture, covering it completely. Place pie dish on a baking tray and heat in a hot oven at 200°C (400°F) for 20-30 minutes or until bubbling hot and browned on top. Serve hot with buttered carrots or a green vegetable.

# Lentil Potato Pie

*Serves 4.*

**Filling:**
**250 g (1¼ cups) lentils**
**1 onion, chopped**
**1 tomato, chopped**
**1 tablespoon chopped parsley**
**1 teaspoon kelp**

**Topping:**
**750 g (1½ lb) potatoes**
**30 g (1 tablespoon) margarine**
**2 tablespoons milk**
**pinch of pepper**

*Filling:* Wash lentils thoroughly in a sieve under cold running water. Place in a heavy-based pan with onion (chopped in a blender or food processor) and sufficient water to cover. Boil uncovered until lentils are tender and water has been absorbed. Cool mixture, then mix to a purée in a blender or food processor. Prepare tomato and parsley in either a blender or a food processor. Stir into lentil mixture with kelp.

*Topping:* Peel potatoes in the Kenwood potato peeler attachment, then cook in boiling salted water until tender. Drain potatoes, then mash in the Kenwood mixer with the K beater. Add margarine, milk and pepper and mix until soft and creamy.

*To finish pie:* Place filling in a greased pie dish. Spread or pipe creamed potato on top. Bake pie in the centre of a moderately hot oven at 190°C (375°F) for 20 minutes or until potato is crisp and brown. Serve hot accompanied by mixed salads.

# Shepherd's Pie

*Serves 4.*

**Filling:**
**500 g (4 cups) chopped cooked beef**
**1 onion, finely chopped**
**3 tablespoons oil or dripping**
**1 tablespoon plain flour**
**250 ml (1 cup) water**
**1 beef stock cube**
**2 tablespoons tomato sauce or paste**
**1 tablespoon chopped parsley**
**½ teaspoon salt**
**¼ teaspoon pepper**

**Topping:**
**750 g (1½ lb) potatoes**
**60 g (2 tablespoons) butter or margarine**
**125 ml (½ cup) milk**

*Filling:* Mince beef in a Kenwood mincer attachment or food processor. Gently fry onion (chopped in a blender or food processor) and beef in hot oil in a large frying pan, stirring occasionally, until all meat is browned. Stir in flour and cook gently for 1 minute. Add water, crumbled stock cube, tomato sauce, parsley, salt, pepper and minced beef. Bring to the boil, then simmer gently until mixture thickens, about 10-15 minutes.

*Topping:* Peel potatoes in a Kenwood potato peeler attachment. Cook potatoes in boiling salted water, drain, place in Kenwood bowl and mash with the K beater, then beat in the butter and milk until creamy.

*To finish pie:* Place filling in a pie dish. Spread creamed potatoes over meat and decorate with a fork. Place pie dish on a baking tray and bake in a hot oven at 200°C (400°F) for 25-30 minutes or until pie is hot and golden brown on top. Serve hot with a green vegetable and buttered carrots.

# PARTY PIES

A hostess who enjoys baking pies couldn't entertain in a more delightful way than serving party pies straight from the oven. A batch of home-made hot savoury pies served along with nuts and olives and a glass of sherry is a delicious pre-dinner savoury. For a cocktail party, a selection of two or three small savoury pies is always popular fare.

You would be an ambitious cook to serve all the following pies at one party, but what about making 'Pies' the theme of your next buffet party? Serve a mixed selection of interesting ethnic favourites such as Russian Pirozhki, Latvian Piragi, Greek Cheese Tricorns, Swiss Mushroom and Tomato Tarts with salad and red and rosé wines. Your guests will love them!

# Tips

Many party pie recipes may be made in advance and frozen in preparation for your party.

Try chopping bacon in the Kenwood blender—it chops it finely (rind and bones removed first) in 3 seconds at minimum speed.

# Russian Pirozhki

*Makes 40.*

**500 g (double quantity) short crust pastry (see page 11)**

*Filling:*
**500 g (1 lb) finely minced lean beef, topside or sirloin**
**2 small onions, finely chopped**
**3 hard-boiled eggs, finely chopped**
**6 tablespoons finely chopped dill *or***
**2 tablespoons dried dill**
**60 g (2 tablespoons) butter**
**1 teaspoon salt**
**¼ teaspoon freshly ground black pepper**

Make pastry according to recipe but double the quantity of butter used, and chill well.

*Filling:* Mince beef in the Kenwood mincer attachment or a food processor. Chop onion, eggs and dill in either a blender or a food processor. Melt butter in a large, heavy frying pan and gently fry onion for 5 minutes until soft and transparent. Stir in the beef and cook until it turns brown. Place beef mixture in a mixing bowl, add egg, dill, salt and pepper and mix well.

*To finish pirozhki:* Shape pastry dough into a rectangle 2.5 cm (1 inch) thick on a floured board and roll out to a 45 x 15 cm (18 x 6 inch) rectangle. Fold dough into three layers, as for making flaky and rough puff pastries, then turn pastry around a quarter turn and roll out again to a 45 x 15 cm rectangle. Fold pastry dough into three layers, then roll and fold twice more as above. Wrap pastry dough in greaseproof paper and chill in refrigerator for at least 1 hour. Roll pastry out to 3 mm (⅛ inch) thick and cut out circles with an 8 cm (3½ inch) pastry cutter. Gather scraps of pastry together, knead lightly, roll out again and cut out as many circles as possible. You should have approx. 40 circles. Place 1 tablespoon filling on centre of each circle. Fold one side of pastry over filling, nearly covering it, fold in both ends approx. 1 cm (½ inch), then brush remaining side with cold water and fold over, sealing well. Place pirozhki, seam side down, on a baking tray and bake in a hot oven at 200°C (400°F) for 30 minutes or until golden brown. Transfer to a wire cooling tray to cool. Serve warm with pre-dinner drinks or with soup or for a snack or a packed lunch.

# Bacon and Egg Tartlets

*Makes 20-24.*

**250 g (1 quantity) shortcrust pastry (see page 11)**

*Filling:*
**125 g (4 oz) bacon rashers**
**2 x 60 g eggs**
**125 ml (½ cup) cream**
**60 g (½ cup) Cheddar cheese, grated**
**¼ teaspoon ground nutmeg**
**pinch of salt**
**pinch of cayenne**

Make pastry according to recipe and chill well.

*Filling:* Remove rind and any bones from bacon with kitchen scissors, chop bacon finely in a blender or food processor. Fry bacon in a hot, heavy frying pan in its own fat until crisp, then drain well. Beat eggs with cream, cheese, nutmeg, salt and cayenne.

*To finish tartlets:* Roll pastry out thinly on a lightly floured board. Cut out rounds with a pastry cutter and place in tartlet tins. Prick tartlets well and bake blind in a hot oven at 220°C (425°F) for 10-15 minutes. Place a little fried bacon in each tartlet and pour egg mixture over. Return to oven for 10-15 minutes, until filling is puffed and golden. Remove from tartlet tins and serve immediately as a party savoury.

# Bacon and Onion Piragi

*Makes 24.*

**500 g (double quantity) piragi dough (see page 16)**

*Filling:*
**250 g (8 oz) bacon**
**1 small onion, finely chopped**
**freshly ground black pepper**
**beaten egg to glaze**

Make dough according to recipe.

*Filling:* Remove rind and any bones from bacon and chop bacon finely in a blender or food processor. Mix chopped bacon with chopped onion (prepared in a blender or food processor) in a heavy frying pan and gently fry for 3-5 minutes, until bacon is transparent. Season with black pepper, drain well and leave to cool.

*To finish piragi:* Roll dough out on a lightly floured board until 5 mm (¼ inch) thick. Cut out 8 cm (3 inch) rounds with a pastry cutter, place a teaspoon of bacon mixture in centre of each, fold in half and press and knead edge to seal well. Pull gently into a crescent shape and place on a greased baking tray, with the join underneath. Cover and leave in a warm place for 10-15 minutes until the piragi are double in size. Make the leftover dough into more piragi, as directed, kneading the scraps together before rerolling. Brush the risen piragi with beaten egg and bake towards the top of a hot oven at 230°C (450°F) for 10-15 minutes, until cooked and golden brown. Serve warm as a party savoury.

# Beef and Cabbage Piragi

*Makes 20-24.*

**250 g (1 quantity) piragi dough (see page 16)**

*Filling:*
**1 onion, finely chopped**
**1 cup finely shredded white cabbage**
**250 g (8 oz) minced beef topside**
**2 hard-boiled eggs, chopped**
**¼ cup finely chopped fresh dill**
**90 g (3 tablespoons) butter or margarine**
**60 ml (¼ cup) sour cream**
**salt**
**freshly ground black pepper**
**beaten egg to glaze**

Make dough according to recipe.

*Filling:* Prepare onion, cabbage, beef, hard-boiled egg and dill in a food processor. In a large heavy-based frying pan, gently fry onion and cabbage in butter over a medium heat for 5 minutes. Add minced beef and cook, stirring frequently, until beef has browned. Stir in hard-boiled eggs, dill, sour cream and salt and pepper to taste. Remove from heat and allow mixture to cool.

*To finish piragi:* On a lightly floured board, roll dough out until 3 mm (⅛ inch) thick. With an 8 cm (3 inch) round cutter, cut out rounds. Place 2 teaspoons of beef filling in centre of each round, pull edges of dough together over filling and pinch edges together to seal. Place pies seam side down on a lightly greased baking tray. Brush pies with beaten egg and bake in a hot oven at 200°C (400°F) for 30 minutes or until golden. Serve warm as a party savoury.

# Cheese and Chutney Tartlets

*Makes 12.*

125 g (½ quantity) short crust pastry (see page 11)

**Filling:**
1 cup mashed banana
60 g (½ cup) Cheddar cheese, grated
2 tablespoons fruit chutney

Prepare pastry according to recipe and chill well.

*Filling:* Mix all ingredients together.

*To finish tartlets:* Roll out pastry 3 mm (⅛ inch) thick, cut out 12 small rounds and line 12 tartlet tins. Place 1-2 teaspoons filling into each pastry tartlet. Bake towards the top of a hot oven at 220°C (425°F) for 12-15 minutes or until cooked and filling is browned. Cool on a wire cooling tray. Serve warm for a party savoury.

# Smoked Fish Pyramids

*Makes 24.*

185 g (1 quantity) cheese pastry (see page 13)

**Filling:**
60 g (½ cup) Cheddar cheese, grated
250 g (8 oz) cooked, smoked fish, cod or haddock
4 egg yolks
1 tablespoon butter, melted
pinch of pepper
cayenne pepper for sprinkling

Make pastry according to recipe and chill well.

*Filling:* Grate cheese in a food processor. Remove skin and bones from fish and discard. Add fish to cheese in food pro-

cessor and mix until flaked. Add egg yolks, butter and pepper and mix until evenly combined.

*To finish pyramids:* Roll pastry out thinly and cut into rounds. Place a teaspoon of filling in centre of each round, brush edges with cold water then bring three sides of circle upwards and seal into a pyramid shape. Place on a greased baking tray and brush with beaten egg. Bake towards the top of a moderate oven at 180°C (350°F) for 15 minutes. Serve warm sprinkled with cayenne pepper as a party savoury.

# Cheese Tricorns

*Makes 40.*

10 sheets phyllo pastry
250 g (1 cup) butter

**Filling:**
250 g (1 cup) cream cheese
125 g (½ cup) feta cheese
90 g (¾ cup) Gruyère cheese, grated
1 x 60 g egg
3 tablespoons chopped parsley

Unwrap phyllo pastry and stack 10 sheets between two clean, cold, damp tea towels. Melt butter over a low heat.

*Filling:* Mix cream cheese and feta cheese together in a food processor or blender until soft. Add grated Gruyére cheese (prepared in a food processor), egg and parsley (chopped in a blender or food processor) and beat well.

*To finish tricorns:* Place 1 sheet phyllo pastry on a pastry board, brush with melted butter, then cut pastry into 8 cm (3 inch) strips. Place a heaped teaspoon of filling in a lower corner of each strip, then fold the phyllo over the filling to form a triangle. Continue folding the strip of phyllo over the filling, keeping the triangle shape, until all the pastry is wrapped around the filling. Place the triangle on a greased baking tray. Continue to shape more triangles with the remaining pastry and filling. Brush the triangles with melted butter and bake in a moderately hot oven at 190°C (375°F) for 20 minutes or until puffed and golden. Serve warm. The tricorns may be allowed to cool, then reheated before serving. A delicious party savoury with drinks.

# Mushroom Tricorns

*Makes 40.*

**20 sheets phyllo pastry**
**250 g (1 cup) butter**

*Filling:*
**60g (¼ cup) butter**
**½ cup thinly sliced shallots**
**500 g (1 lb) mushrooms, chopped**
**extra 30 g (1 tablespoon) butter**
**30 g (2 tablespoons) plain flour**
**½ teaspoon curry powder**
**½ teaspoon salt**
**freshly ground black pepper**
**250 ml (1 cup) cream**

Unwrap phyllo pastry and layer 20 sheets between two clean, cold, damp tea towels. Melt butter in a pan over a low heat.

*Filling:* Heat butter in a frying pan and fry shallots and mushrooms (both prepared in a food processor) over a medium-high heat, stirring occasionally, until mushrooms are soft. Reduce heat, add extra butter and heat until melted. Stir in flour, curry powder, salt and pepper over a medium heat for 1-2 minutes. Remove from heat, stir in cream, then return to heat and stir continuously until mixture thickens and just comes to the boil. Remove from heat and leave to cool.

*To finish tricorns:* Brush 1 sheet of phyllo pastry with melted butter, then cut in half lengthways with kitchen scissors. Fold each half in half lengthways and brush each with more butter. Place 1 tablespoon mushroom filling in a lower corner of each strip, then fold the phyllo over the filling to form a triangle and continue folding over and shaping as for Cheese Tricorns (see page 63). Continue shaping triangles in this method and place on a greased baking tray. Brush triangles with melted butter and bake in a moderately hot oven at 190°C (375°F) for 20-25 minutes or until puffed and golden. Serve warm as a party savoury.

# Mushroom and Tomato Tarts

*Makes 12 tarts.*

**185 g (1 quantity) pâte brisée (see page 12)**

*Filling:*
**125 g (4 oz) button mushrooms, coarsely chopped**
**1 cup finely chopped shallots**
**2 tomatoes, peeled, seeded and chopped**
**1 tablespoon oil**
**4 anchovy fillets**
**¼ teaspoon salt**
**¼ teaspoon dried thyme**
**¼ teaspoon freshly grated or ground nutmeg**
**freshly ground black pepper**
**2 x 60 g eggs**
**165 ml ( ⅔ cup) cream**

Make pâte brisée according to recipe and chill well.

*Filling:* Prepare mushrooms, shallots and tomatoes in a food processor. Heat oil in a heavy frying pan and gently fry mushrooms for 5 minutes, add shallots and stir over heat until softened. Add tomatoes and cook mixture, stirring occasionally until liquid begins to evaporate. Drain anchovy fillets, rinse, pat dry, then chop. Stir anchovy fillets into vegetable mixture with salt, thyme, nutmeg and pepper to taste. Cook over a medium heat, stirring, until liquid has evaporated. Transfer to a shallow dish and allow to cool. Whisk eggs in an electric mixer until light and fluffy, then whisk in cream. Stir egg mixture into the cooled vegetable mixture.

*To finish tarts:* Roll out pastry on a lightly floured board into a large circle about 3 mm (⅛ inch) thick. Using a 9 cm (3½ inch) pastry cutter, cut out 12 rounds. Line 12 x 8 cm (3 inch) fluted tartlet tins with pastry rounds. Prick bottom of each tart case with a fork, then place on a baking tray. Cut out 12 rounds of greaseproof paper and line each tart case with a round of paper, then cover with a layer of baking beans. Bake 'blind' towards the top of a hot oven at 200°C (400°F) for 10 minutes. Remove greaseproof paper and baking beans ('blind' filling), return tart cases to oven and continue to bake for a further 10 minutes. Remove tins from baking tray and place on a wire cooling tray to cool. Return tart cases (in tins) to baking tray. Carefully spoon about 2 tablespoons of filling into each tart case. Bake towards the top of a moderately hot oven at 190°C (375°F) for 20 minutes or until set and puffed. Serve tarts immediately for a party savoury.

Fruit Tartlets and Apricot and Almond Flan *(see pages 85, 80)*

# Sausage Rolls

*Makes 12-14.*

**250 g (1 quantity) puff, rough puff or flaky pastry (see pages 15, 16)**

*Filling:*
**250 g (8 oz) sausage meat**
**beaten egg to glaze**

Make pastry as directed in recipe and chill well.

*Filling:* Divide sausage meat in half and roll each half into a long thin roll, 35 cm (14 inches) long, on a lightly floured board. Put to one side.

*To finish rolls:* Roll pastry out to an oblong 35 cm (14 inches) long and 25 cm (10 inches) wide, cut in half lengthways to make two long strips. Place rolls of sausage meat on one side of each pastry strip. Brush long edges of pastry strips with cold water and fold pastry over sausage, join edges together and press to seal, but leave ends open. Seal and flake edges with a round-bladed knife. Cut each roll into 6 or 7 sausage rolls and make three diagonal slits on top of each. Place rolls on a baking tray and chill in refrigerator for 10-15 minutes. Brush rolls with beaten egg and bake in the top of a very hot oven at 230°C (450°F) for 25-30 minutes or until pastry is crisp and golden and sausage meat is cooked. Cool on a wire cooling tray. Serve warm as a party savoury.

Rhubarb Flan
*(see page 84)*

# FRUIT PIES

Apple pie is one of the most popular puddings to have come out of England. In America they now say 'as American as apple pie' and, thanks to the early settlers and a lady called 'Granny Smith', an apple pie is equally popular in Australia.

A fruit pie is usually made in a deep oval dish or a deep round plate. Sometimes the dish or plate is lined with pastry, then filled with fruit and covered with more pastry, and at other times the fruit goes straight into the unlined dish and is covered with a layer of pastry.

Traditionally fruit pies have flaked edges with scallops approx. 1 cm (½ inch) apart, the tops are left plain and they are either left unglazed or they are glazed with lightly whisked egg white and castor sugar. In this way you can identify a fruit pie from a meat pie.

There are detailed instructions for covering a fruit pie in the correct traditional method in the recipe for Apple Pie.

# Tips

Always make two slits opposite each other between the rim of the pie dish and the pastry to allow the steam from the fruit to escape.

Never sprinkle sugar on top of the fruit— place it in the middle of the filling. Sugar touching the underside of the pastry crust turns it soggy.

# Apple Pie

*Serves 4-6.*

**185 g (1 quantity) sweet short crust pastry (see page 11)**

*Filling:*
**625 g (approx. 5 medium) green cooking apples**
**60 g (¼ cup) sugar**
**1 tablespoon water**
**egg white and castor sugar to glaze**

Prepare sweet short crust pastry according to recipe and chill until required.

*Filling:* Peel apples, cut into quarters, remove cores and slice half the apples into a 1 litre (4 cup) pie dish. Sprinkle with sugar and 1 tablespoon water and cover with remaining sliced apple, shaping them into a dome. (If sugar touches pastry it makes it soft and sticky underneath.)

*To finish pie:* Roll pastry out to an oval shape large enough to cover pie dish. Continue rolling until pastry has a 2.5 cm (1 inch) margin bigger than top of dish. Cut a 1 cm (½ inch) rim off pastry. Brush rim of pie dish with cold water and press pastry rim on top, trim ends so they meet without overlapping. Brush pastry rim with cold water, then place remaining pastry over apples and ease pastry in carefully, to avoid shrinkage during baking. Press pastry onto rim to seal, then trim edges with a sharp knife with the blade angled away from pie's edge. This also avoids shrinkage. Flake or 'knock-up' edge of pie with a round-bladed knife, cutting pastry with your little finger flat behind the edge. Scallop or flute edges at 1 cm (½ inch) intervals. Make a neat round hole in top of pastry with a skewer. Slide a small knife between rim of pie dish and pastry at either end of pie. This prevents filling bubbling over on to centre of pastry when steam escapes. Glaze with lightly beaten egg white and sprinkle with castor sugar. Place pie dish on a baking tray and bake towards the top of a hot oven at 220°C (425°F) for 15 minutes or until pastry is crisp and golden. Reduce heat to moderately slow at 160°C (325°F) and continue baking until fruit is cooked, about 15 minutes more. Steam coming out of centre hole shows that the fruit is cooked. Serve apple pie hot with custard or pouring cream.

# Apple Amber Pie

*Serves 6-8.*

**250 g (1 quantity) short crust pastry (see page 11)**

*Filling:*
**500 g (1 lb) cooking apples**
**60 g (¼ cup) sugar**
**finely grated rind and juice of 1 lemon**
**30 g (1 tablespoon) soft butter or margarine**
**1 x 60 g egg**
**castor sugar for sprinkling**

Make pastry according to recipe and chill well.

*Filling:* Peel, core and slice apples into a clean pan. Add sugar, rind and juice of lemon, cover and stew gently for 10 minutes. Stir butter or margarine into apples. Separate egg and stir egg yolk into apple mixture.

*To finish pie:* Roll half pastry out on a lightly floured board to a round 3 mm (⅛ inch) thick, and line a 20 cm (8 inch) flan tin with a loose bottom, or 20 cm (8 inch) flan ring placed on a baking tray. Place filling in pastry and brush edge with cold water. Roll out remaining half of pastry to a round 3 mm (⅛ inch) thick and place on top of apples. Seal, trim and decorate edge. Make a slit in the top of the pie to allow steam to escape. Whisk egg white very lightly, brush over top of pie and sprinkle with castor sugar. Bake towards the top of a hot oven at 200°C (400°F) for 15-20 minutes or until pastry is cooked and golden brown. Serve hot or cold with custard or whipped cream.

# Apple Streusal Pie

*Serves 8.*

*Pastry:*
**185 g (1½ cups) plain flour**
**125 g (½ cup) butter, chilled**
**50 g (½ cup) rolled oats**
**2 tablespoons sugar**
**finely grated rind of 1 lemon**
**1 egg yolk**
**2-3 tablespoons water**
**egg white to glaze**

*Filling:*
**1 kg (2 lb) cooking apples**
**1 tablespoon lemon juice**
**90 g (½ cup) sultanas**
**90 g (½ cup) brown sugar**
**½ teaspoon ground cinnamon**

*Topping:*
**30 g (1 tablespoon) butter**
**2 tablespoons brown sugar**
**2 tablespoons plain flour**
**25 g (¼ cup) rolled oats**

*Pastry:* Sift flour into Kenwood bowl. Cut butter into small cubes, add to flour and beat with K beater at speed 1 for 30 seconds. Slowly increase to speed 3 and beat for 1½ minutes longer. Add rolled oats, sugar and lemon rind, mix for 10 seconds to combine, then add egg yolk and water gradually and mix to a firm dough at speed 1, increasing to speed 2 until dough leaves sides of bowl cleanly.

*Filling:* Peel, core and slice apples thinly. Place in a bowl and sprinkle with lemon juice. Add sultanas, brown sugar and ground cinnamon and mix gently.

*Topping:* Place all ingredients in blender or food processor and blend briefly, just until crumbly.

*To finish pie:* On a lightly floured board, roll out pastry to a thin round and line a 23 cm (9 inch) pie plate and decorate edge. Prick base of pastry and glaze all over with lightly beaten egg white. Place filling carefully into pastry case, shaping it into a dome in the centre. Sprinkle topping over filling. Stand pie on a baking tray and bake in a hot oven at 200°C (400°F) for 10 minutes. Reduce temperature to moderate at 180°C (350°F) for a further 40 minutes, or until apples are just tender. Serve Apple Streusal Pie either hot or cold with whipped cream.

# Dutch Apple Pie

*Serves 8.*

*Pastry:*
**185 g (1½ cups) plain flour**
**1 teaspoon baking powder**
**90 g (3 tablespoons) butter or margarine**
**1 small egg**
**3 tablespoons castor sugar**
**1 teaspoon vanilla essence**

*Filling:*
**125 ml (½ cup) golden syrup**
**1 x 60 g egg**
**3 medium cooking apples**
**60 g (⅓ cup) chopped dates**
**30 g (1 tablespoon) butter**

*Pastry:* Sift flour and baking powder into Kenwood bowl, add butter, egg, sugar and vanilla all together and mix at speed 1 for 5 seconds, then gradually increase speed to 3 and beat for 25 seconds until dough comes together.

*Filling:* Melt golden syrup over a gentle heat, remove from heat and beat in the egg. Peel and core the apples, then cut into thin slices.

*To finish pie:* Roll pastry out to a round on a lightly floured board and line a lightly greased 23 cm (9 inch) pie plate. Pour half the syrup and egg mixture over pastry, arrange the apple slices on top, then pour remaining syrup mixture over. Scatter chopped dates over the top and dot with butter. Bake pie in a hot oven at 200°C (400°F) for 5 minutes, reduce heat to moderately hot at 190°C (375°F) and bake for a further 30-35 minutes. Serve warm with whipped cream or stirred egg custard.

# Healthy Apple Pie

*Serves 6-8.*

**250 g (1 quantity) wholemeal pastry (see page 13)**

*Filling:*
**5 medium cooking apples**
**60 g (⅓ cup) sultanas**
**2 tablespoons lemon juice**
**3 tablespoons honey**
**¼ teaspoon ground cinnamon**
**¼ teaspoon mixed spice**
**½ cup sliced rhubarb**

**4 tablespoons water**
**milk to glaze**
**1 tablespoon wheatgerm and 2 teaspoons raw sugar for sprinkling**

Make pastry according to recipe but use milk in place of water and chill well.

*Filling:* Peel, core and slice apples and place in a large pan. Add sultanas, lemon juice, honey, spices, rhubarb and water. Cook over a gentle heat until apples and rhubarb are tender. Allow to cool.

*To finish pie:* Roll half pastry out to a round and line a 23 cm (9 inch) pie plate as for Blackberry and Apple Pie (see page 69). Spoon cool apple filling into pastry case. Roll out remaining pastry and cover pie. Seal, trim, flake and scallop edge of pastry. Brush top of pie with extra milk and sprinkle with wheatgerm and raw sugar. Bake towards the top of a very hot oven at 220°C (425°F) for about 15 minutes or until pastry is cooked. Serve hot with natural yoghurt or whipped cream.

# Hungarian Apple Pie

*Serves 8.*

**375 g (double quantity) rich short crust pastry (see page 12)**

*Filling:*
**4 large cooking apples**
**3 tablespoons sugar**
**1 lemon**
**60 g (½ cup) ground almonds**
**1 egg white**
**4 tablespoons cherry or raspberry jam**
**egg white and sugar for glazing**
**whipped cream for serving**

Make pastry according to recipe but use sour cream in place of cold water. Chill well.

*Filling:* Peel, core and slice apples into a pan. Add 1 tablespoon sugar, strips of lemon rind and juice of lemon. Cover and stew gently until apples have fallen to a purée. Leave to cool. Mix remaining sugar with ground almonds. Whisk egg white until stiff and fold into the cold apple purée.

*To finish pie:* Roll out half pastry to a round shape and line a round 23 cm (9 inch) pie plate. Spread jam over the base and sprinkle half the sugar and almond mixture on top. Spread apple purée on top and sprinkle with remaining sugar and almond mixture. Roll out remaining pastry to a round shape. Brush rim of pie with cold water and place round of pastry on top. Press edges together to seal, then trim, flake and decorate edge. Brush pie with lightly beaten egg white and sprinkle sugar over top. Place pie on a baking tray and bake in a hot oven at 220°C (425°F) for 30 minutes or until pastry is cooked and golden brown. Serve pie warm with whipped cream.

## Blackberry and Apple Pie

*Serves 8.*

**375 g (double quantity) sweet short crust pastry (see page 11)**

*Filling:*
**5 large cooking apples**
**500 g (1 lb) fresh *or* 1 x 380 g can blackberries**
**2 tablespoons sugar**
**egg white and castor sugar for glazing**
**icing sugar for sprinkling**

Make pastry according to recipe and chill for 30 minutes.

*Filling:* Cut apples into quarters, remove peel and core and slice apple into thick segments. Pick over fresh blackberries, or drain canned blackberries.

*To finish pie:* Roll half pastry out on a lightly floured board to a round shape and place in the bottom of a round 23 cm (9 inch) pie plate. Press pastry into place with the back of your fingers, trim overlapping edge off with a sharp knife and prick the base. Place half the apple in the pastry case and sprinkle with half the sugar. Cover with blackberries, remaining sugar and apple, shaping the fruit into a dome in the centre. Roll out remaining pastry to a round shape large enough to cover pie. Brush edge of pastry rim on pie dish with cold water, then place round of pastry on top. Press edges gently together to seal around the rim, then trim excess pastry off with a sharp knife. Flake or scallop edge of pie with a round-bladed knife and make two holes on top with a skewer to allow steam to escape. Brush pastry with lightly beaten egg white. Roll out pastry scraps and cut small circles out with a special pastry cutter (or the top of a lipstick) and place decoratively on top of pie. Brush circles with egg white and sprinkle pie with sugar. Place pie on a baking tray and bake in a hot oven at 220°C (425°F) for 20-30 minutes, until pastry is golden brown and cooked. Sift icing sugar over pie before serving. Serve hot or cold with cream, custard or ice cream.

## Rhubarb and Apple Pie

*Serves 4-6.*

**185 g ( 1 quantity) sweet short crust pastry (see page 11)**

*Filling:*
**500 g (1 lb) rhubarb**
**500 g (1 lb) cooking apples**
**3 tablespoons sugar**
**egg white and castor sugar to glaze**

Prepare pastry according to recipe and chill well.

*Filling:* Trim and wash rhubarb in cold water. Cut rhubarb into 2.5 cm (1 inch) pieces. Peel, quarter and core apples. Slice apples into an oval pie dish, layering them with the rhubarb and sugar.

*To finish pie:* Roll pastry out to an oval and cover pie as directed in Apple Pie (see page 66). Brush pie with lightly beaten egg white and sprinkle with castor sugar and stand on a baking tray. Bake towards the top of a hot oven at 220°C (425°F) for 20-30 minutes until golden brown and cooked. Serve hot or warm with custard or pouring cream.

# Apple Turnovers

*Serves 6.*

**250 g (1 quantity) puff, rough puff or flaky pastry (see pages 15, 16)**

*Filling:*
**2 large cooking apples**
**1 tablespoon sugar**
**¼ teaspoon ground cinnamon**
**egg white and castor sugar to glaze**

Make pastry as directed and chill well.

*Filling:* Peel, core and dice apples. Mix with sugar and cinnamon.

*To finish turnovers:* Roll pastry out to a 37 x 25 cm (15 x 10 inch) rectangle. Cut into six 12 cm (5 inch) squares. Divide filling between pastry squares. Brush edges with cold water, fold one corner over to meet other to form a triangle, and seal edges. Flake edges with a round-bladed knife. Place turnovers on a damp baking tray and chill in refrigerator for 20 minutes. Brush turnovers with lightly beaten egg white and sprinkle with castor sugar. Bake at the top of a hot oven at 220°C (425°F) for 20 minutes or until crisp and golden brown. Serve hot with custard or pouring cream.

**Variation:** Substitute 2 cups chopped apricots or peaches for apple filling.

# Apricot Pie

*Serves 8.*

**375 g (double quantity) sweet short crust pastry (see page 11)**

*Filling:*
**1 kg (2 lb) fresh apricots, halved, or 1 x 825 g can apricots**
**1 cup apricot jam**
**1 lemon**
**egg white and castor sugar for glazing**
**icing sugar for sprinkling**

Make pastry according to recipe and chill well.

*Filling:* Drain apricots if using canned fruit.

*To finish pie:* Roll half pastry out on a lightly floured board to a round shape and line a round 23 cm (9 inch) pie plate. Trim edge and prick base. Place apricots into pastry case, cover with apricot jam, then grate lemon rind on top and sprinkle lemon juice over. Roll out remaining pastry to a round shape and cover pie as for Blackberry and Apple Pie (see page 66). Brush pie with lightly beaten egg white and sprinkle sugar over top. Place pie on a baking tray and bake in a hot oven at 220°C (425°F) for 20-30 minutes or until pastry is cooked and golden brown. Serve pie warm, sprinkled with icing sugar, with whipped cream, custard or ice cream.

# Fruit Salad Ring

*Serves 6.*

**60 g (1 quantity) choux pastry (see page 15)**

*Filling:*
**1 orange, peeled and segmented**
**1 apple, peeled, cored and cut into 1 cm (½ inch) cubes**
**1 banana, peeled, sliced and sprinkled with lemon juice**
**½ pawpaw, peeled, seeded and cut into 1 cm (½ inch) cubes**
**pulp of 2 passionfruit**
**300 ml (1 jar/carton) cream, whipped**

*Pastry:* Make pastry according to recipe and place in metal tablespoonfuls on a ligthly greased baking tray to form a circle. With the back of the spoon, join all spoonfuls of pastry together. Bake in a hot oven at 220°C (425°F) for 30 minutes, then reduce to moderately hot at 190°C (375°F) and cook for a further 20 minutes. Transfer to a wire cooling tray and split ring in half horizontally using a serrated bread knife and leave to cool.

*Filling:* Prepare fruit as directed, place in a mixing bowl and fold together gently.

*To finish ring:* Place bottom half of pastry ring on a serving plate and fill with fruit salad. Spoon whipped cream over fruit, then place top half of choux ring on top. Serve immediately.

# Mince Pies

*Makes 24.*

**Pastry:**
**315 g (2½ cups) plain flour**
**155 g (5 tablespoons) butter**
**30 g (¼ cup) ground almonds**
**90 g (3 tablespoons) castor sugar**
**2 egg yolks**
**lemon juice or cold water to mix**

**Filling:**
**250 g (1 cup) fruit mincemeat**
**2 tablespoons brandy or rum**
**icing sugar for sprinkling**

*Pastry:* Sift flour into the Kenwood bowl, add butter, cut into small pieces and mix at speed 2 until mixture resembles bread-crumbs. Add ground almonds, castor sugar, egg yolks and sufficient lemon juice or cold water and mix to a stiff dough. Knead lightly, wrap in greaseproof paper and chill for 30 minutes.

*Filling:* Mix fruit mincemeat with brandy or rum.

*To finish pies:* Roll pastry out on a lightly floured board to 3 mm (⅛ inch) thick and cut out 24 rounds, large enough to line tartlet tins, and 24 smaller tops, with pastry cutters. Place large pastry rounds firmly into tartlet tins and place a teaspoon of fruit mincemeat in each. Brush edge of tartlets with cold water and place pastry tops on, sealing carefully around edge. Make two neat holes with a skewer, or two snips with kitchen scissors, on top of each pie. Alternatively, you may cut out a star shape with a small star pastry cutter from the pastry tops before finishing pies. Bake at the top of a hot oven at 220°C (425°F) for 15-20 minutes or until cooked and golden. Serve warm, sprinkled with sifted icing sugar.

**Note:** You may make and bake these in advance, deep-freeze or store in an airtight tin for 2 weeks and reheat before serving.

**Variation:** Mince pies may also be made from short crust pastry or flaky pastry or rough puff pastry, but this pastry is particularly delicious.

# Mince Tart

*Serves 6-8.*

**185 g (1 quantity) sweet short crust or one-stage short crust pastry (see pages 11, 12)**

**Filling:**
**2 cups fruit mincemeat**
**1 cup stewed apple**
**beaten egg and castor sugar to glaze**
**icing sugar for sprinkling**

Make pastry according to recipe and chill well.

*Filling:* Mix fruit mincemeat and stewed apple together.

*To finish tart:* Roll three-quarters of pastry out on a lightly floured board to a thin round and line a 23 cm (9 inch) pie plate. Prick base of pastry case and chill for 30 minutes. Spread filling in pastry case. Roll remaining pastry out thinly to a rectangle 20 cm (8 inches) long, cut it into 10 mm (½ inch) strips and place on top of filling in a lattice design. Trim strips from edge and decorate edge by pinching a finger between the finger and thumb of the other hand. Place on a baking tray and bake towards the top of a moderate oven at 180°C (350°F) for 25 minutes or until cooked. Serve warm or cold with whipped cream or ice cream.

# Mulberry Pie

*Serves 8.*

**375 g (double quantity) sweet short crust pastry (see page 11)**

**Filling:**
**750 g (1½ lb) mulberries**
**2 tablespoons sugar**
**egg white and castor sugar to glaze**

Make pastry according to recipe and chill for 30 minutes.

*Filling:* Pick over mulberries to remove any stems and rinse under cold running water.

*To finish pie:* Finish pie as for Blackberry and Apple Pie (see page 69), omitting icing sugar. Serve hot or cold with cream or ice cream.

# Peach Cobbler

*Serves 8.*

*Pastry:*
**125 g (½ cup) butter**
**60 g (¼ cup) castor sugar**
**2 x 60 g eggs**
**250 g (2 cups) plain flour**
**1 teaspoon cream of tartar**
**¼ teaspoon bicarbonate of soda**
**pinch of salt**
**150 ml milk**

*Filling:*
**3 tablespoons tapioca, soaked in cold water overnight**
**90 g (3 tablespoons) butter**
**185 g (¾ cup) sugar**
**8 fresh peaches, peeled, stoned and sliced, or 1 x 825 g can sliced peaches, drained**
**150 ml (½ jar/carton) cream**
**cherries and angelica for decoration**

*Pastry:* Place butter and castor sugar in the Kenwood bowl and cream with the K beater on speed 1 for 30 seconds, then increase to speed 5 for 2 minutes. Add eggs, one at a time, and beat at speed 5 for 30 seconds after each one is added. Sift flour, cream of tartar, bicarbonate of soda and salt together. Add to basic mixture, alternating with milk, and mix at speed 3 for 5 seconds after each addition.

*Filling:* Drain soaked tapioca and place in a small pan with butter and sugar. Cover and stew over a low heat until tender, then leave to cool.

*To finish cobbler:* Spoon half pastry mixture into a greased round 23 cm (9 inch) pie plate and spread smooth. Spread tapioca mixture over pastry dough and arrange sliced peaches on top. Spread the remaining pastry dough over the peaches. Bake towards the top of a moderately hot oven at 190°C (375°F) for 30 minutes or until golden brown. Serve warm or cold decorated with rosettes of whipped cream, cherry segments and angelica leaves.

# Peach Pie

*Serves 4-6.*

**185 g (1 quantity) wholemeal wheatgerm pastry, or sweet short crust pastry (see pages 11, 14)**

*Filling:*
**8 fresh sliced peaches or 1 x 825 g can sliced peaches**
**2 tablespoons tapioca**
**egg white and castor sugar to glaze**

Prepare pastry as directed in recipe and chill well.

*Filling:* If using canned peaches, drain peaches and reserve juice. Layer sliced peaches with tapioca in a 1 litre (4 cup) oval pie dish.

*To finish pie:* Roll pastry out to an oval and cover pie as directed for Apple Pie (page 66). Make a slit at either end of rim and a hole in the centre with a skewer to allow steam to escape. Brush pastry with lightly beaten egg white and sprinkle with castor sugar. Stand pie dish on a baking tray and bake towards the top of a hot oven at 200°C (400°F) for 20-30 minutes or until pastry is cooked. Serve hot or warm with whipped cream, custard or ice cream.

Pumpkin Pie and Egg Nog Pie
*(see pages 91, 89)*

# Pear Pie

*Serves 6.*

**250 g (1 quantity) rich short crust pastry
(see page 12)**

*Filling:*
**2 large dessert pears
1 tablespoon castor sugar
finely grated rind and juice of 1 orange
2 tablespoons brandy
egg white and castor sugar to glaze**

Make pastry according to recipe and chill
well.

*Filling:* Peel, quarter and core the pears
and place in a single layer in a large
shallow dish. Sprinkle with castor sugar,
orange rind and juice and brandy. Cover
and macerate for 30 minutes.

*To finish pie:* Roll a third of the pastry out
to a 20 cm (8 inch) round and cut a 6 cm
(2½ inch) round from the centre. Knead
the small round lightly into the remaining
dough, then roll it out to a round and line
a smooth 20 cm (8 inch) flan ring standing
on a baking tray. Drain pears and place
neatly in the pastry case (thin ends towards
the centre). Brush edge of pastry case with
cold water, then cover with the round of
pastry, seal, trim and decorate edges. Bake
towards the top of a moderately hot oven at
190°C (375°F) for 35 minutes. Whisk egg
white very lightly, brush over top of pie and
sprinkle with castor sugar. Return to oven
for a further 5 minutes. Cool pie on a wire
cooling tray. Serve warm or cold with
whipped cream or custard.

# American Plum Pie

*Serves 6-8.*

**250 g (1 quantity) American pastry (see
page 14)**

*Filling:*
**750 g (1½ lb) plums
250 ml (1 cup) water
3 tablespoons sugar
30 g (1 tablespoon) butter or margarine
1 tablespoon sago *or* tapioca
¼ teaspoon almond essence
egg white and castor sugar to glaze**

Make pastry according to recipe and chill
well.

*Filling:* Wash plums in cold water and
place in a heavy pan. Add water and sugar,
then cover and stew gently for 10-15
minutes until tender. Remove from heat,
stir in butter, sago and almond essence
and leave to stand for 15 minutes.

*To finish pie:* Roll half pastry out to a round
and line a round 23 cm (9 inch) pie dish
and trim edge. Pour filling into pastry case.
Roll remaining pastry out to a round and
cover pie, trim and decorate edge as for
Blackberry and Apple Pie (see page 69).
Bake pie towards the top of a hot oven at
220°C (425°F) for 30 minutes. Whisk egg
white until frothy and brush over pie, then
sprinkle castor sugar on top. Return to
oven and bake for a further 5 minutes.
Serve pie hot or cold with whipped cream.

Frangipani Pie
*(see page 93)*

# FRUIT FLANS, TARTS AND TARLETS

Fruit flans, tarts and tartlets always attract me magnetically to a dessert trolly when dining out in a top restaurant because they look so beautiful. Fruit flans, like savoury flans, are open tarts, but they are filled with refreshing seasonal fruits topped with a glaze or baked in a rich custard cream. Tarts tend to have fillings which are made from other ingredients (not fruit) and sometimes have a latticed topping of pastry over the filling.

Tartlets are individual tarts which are baked in either small flan tins or in a tray of tartlet tins; they can be filled with fruit or other delicious fillings.

Most fruit flan cases are baked 'blind', which means baking the pastry case lined with a piece of greaseproof paper and filled with a layer of large dry beans (such as haricot) for about the first 10 minutes, or until the pastry case has set in shape. The 'blind' filling, i.e., the paper and beans, is removed carefully and the flan case is either baked empty until cooked or the filling is placed in the flan case and they are baked together until cooked.

The following recipes will guide you through the art of flan making.

## Tips

Prick pastry cases *lightly* with a fine fork before baking 'blind'. A coarse fork can make holes in the flan case.

Fill flan cases with fruit fillings as close as possible to serving time to retain the texture of the pastry.

## Apricot and Almond Flan

*Serves 6.*

**185 g (¾ quantity) rich short crust pastry or pâte sucrée (see pages 12, 13)**
**4 tablespoons ground almonds**

*Filling:*
**300 ml (1 jar/carton) cream**
**825 g can apricot halves**
**6 tablespoons apricot jam**
**2 teaspoons arrowroot or cornflour**
**blanched toasted almonds**

Make pastry according to recipe, adding almonds with the sugar, and chill well.

*Filling:* Whip cream until thick. Drain apricots well and reserve 125 ml (½ cup) juice. Place apricot juice and jam in a saucepan and dissolve jam over a medium heat. Strain juice and jam mixture and return to saucepan. Blend arrowroot smoothly with a little extra apricot juice, add to saucepan and bring to the boil, stirring continuously until the glaze clears and thickens. Cool but do not allow to set.

*To finish flan:* Roll pastry out thinly and line a 20 cm (8 inch) deep flan tin or a 23 cm (9 inch) shallow flan tin. Bake 'blind' on the top of a hot oven at 220°C (425°F) for 10-15 minutes or until pastry is set in shape. Remove 'blind' filling and bake in a moderately hot oven at 180°C (375°F) for 10-15 minutes or until pastry is cooked. Cool on a wire cooling tray, remove from flan tin after a few minutes then leave until cold. Spread whipped cream over bottom of pastry case, then top neatly with apricot halves. Place toasted almonds between the apricot halves. Brush glaze over fruit and leave to set before serving.

**Variation:** Peach Flan—substitute canned peach slices for apricots.

## Bakewell Tart

*Serves 6.*

**185 g (1 quantity) sweet short crust pastry (see page 11)**

*Filling:*
**90 g (3 tablespoons) soft butter or margarine**

90 g (⅓ cup) castor sugar
2 x 60 g eggs
60 g (¼ cup) ground almonds
60 g (½ cup) self-raising flour, sifted
few drops almond essence
3 tablespoons raspberry jam
6 split almonds for decoration
icing sugar for sprinkling

Prepare pastry according to recipe and chill well.

*Filling:* Place all ingredients, except jam and split almonds, in a mixing bowl and beat well with an electric mixer until well mixed (1-2 minutes).

*To finish tart:* Roll pastry out thinly to a round and line a 20 cm (8 inch) flan tin. Reserve pastry trimmings and prick base of flan. Spread jam over bottom of pastry case, then spread with ground almonds mixture. Roll pastry trimmings into a long strip and cut into strips 1 cm (½ inch) wide; place on tart in a lattice pattern and trim neatly. Decorate top of tart with split almonds. Bake in the middle of a moderate oven at 180°C (350°F) for 45-50 minutes, until cooked. Cool on a wire cooling tray. Serve warm sprinkled with icing sugar for a dessert, accompanied by custard or pouring cream.

# Buttermilk Chess Pie

*Serves 6-8.*

155 g 1 quantity) lard pastry (see page 14)

*Filling:*
60 g (2 tablespoons) butter, softened
250 g (1 cup) castor sugar
3 x 60 g eggs
30 g (¼ cup) flour
¼ teaspoon salt
250 ml (1 cup) buttermilk
1 teaspoon vanilla essence
ground nutmeg for sprinkling

Make pastry according to recipe and chill well.

*Filling:* Place butter and sugar in the Kenwood bowl and cream at speed 4 for 60 seconds. Increase gradually to maximum and continue to beat until mixture is well creamed, scraping down when necessary. Beat in eggs, one at a time, at speed 5. Fold in sifted flour and salt with a metal

tablespoon or spatula. Add buttermilk and vanilla essence in a stream, mixing constantly with the spoon.

*To finish pie:* Roll out pastry to a round and line a 23 cm (9 inch) pie plate or flan tin. Bake 'blind' towards the top of a hot oven at 200°C (400°F) for 10 minutes, remove baking beans and paper ('blind' filling) and bake for a further 10 minutes in a moderately hot oven at 190°C (375°F). Allow to cool slightly. Carefully spoon filling into pastry case and bake in centre of oven at 190°C (375°F) for 30-35 minutes, or until filling is set. Transfer pie plate to a wire cooling tray and allow to cool. Serve Buttermilk Chess Pie warm or cold, sprinkled with ground nutmeg and accompanied by whipped cream.

# Cherry Tart

*Serves 6-8.*

250 g (1 quantity) pâte sucrée (see page 13)

*Filling:*
500 g (1 lb) cherries
60 g (¼ cup) sugar
2 tablespoons kirsch
1 x 60 g egg
2 tablespoons castor sugar
1 teaspoon vanilla essence
3 tablespoons cream
icing sugar for decoration

Make pastry according to recipe and chill well.

*Filling:* Stone cherries, place in a mixing bowl, sprinkle sugar and kirsch over and leave to stand for 1-2 hours. Beat egg with sugar, vanilla and cream.

*To finish tart:* Roll pastry out thinly and line a 23 cm (9 inch) flan tin. Prick base and chill pastry case for ½-1 hour. Transfer cherries with a slotted spoon to the pastry case and bake in the middle of a hot oven at 200°C (400°F) for 25 minutes. Remove tart from oven, pour egg mixture over, then bake tart in the bottom of the oven for a further 20 minutes or until custard is set. Remove tart from oven and sprinkle icing sugar over while warm. Cool on a wire cooling tray. Serve warm or chilled with whipped cream.

# Coffee and Bran Tart

*Serves 6.*

185 g (1 quantity) rich short crust pastry
(see page 12)

*Filling:*
90 g (3 tablespoons) soft butter or
margarine
90 g (3 tablespoons) castor sugar
1 x 60 g egg
60 g (1 cup) all bran
30 g (¼ cup) chopped hazelnuts
125 g (1 cup) self-raising flour
2 teaspoons instant coffee dissolved in 3
teaspoons hot water
60 ml (¼ cup) milk
4 tablespoons apricot or raspberry jam
250 ml (1 cup) sour cream or natural
yoghurt

Make pastry according to recipe and chill
well.

*Filling:* Cream butter and sugar together
in Kenwood bowl until light and fluffy. Add
egg gradually, beating well after each
addition. Stir in all bran and hazelnuts, then
fold in sifted flour alternately with dissolved
coffee and milk.

*To finish tart:* Roll pastry out thinly on a
lightly floured board to a round and line a
20 cm (8 inch) flan tin. Prick base of pastry
case. Spread jam over bottom of pastry
case, then spread coffee mixture over jam.
Bake in the middle of a hot oven at 200°C
(400°F) for 10 minutes, then reduce temperature to moderately slow, 160°C
(325°F), and bake for a further 20 minutes.
Remove tart from oven, quickly spread
sour cream over top and return to oven for
2 minutes. Serve warm.

# French Pear Tart

*Serves 6.*

185 g (¾ quantity) rich short crust pastry
or pâte sucrée (see pages 12, 13)

*Filling:*
3 ripe dessert pears
1 x 60 g egg
2 tablespoons castor sugar
¼ teaspoon salt
⅛ teaspoon ground ginger
⅛ teaspoon ground nutmeg
finely grated rind of 1 lemon
250 ml (1 cup) sour cream

*Topping:*
2 tablespoons plain flour
3 tablespoons brown sugar
60 g (⅓ cup) chilled butter
¼ teaspoon ground nutmeg

Make pastry according to recipe and chill
well.

*Filling:* Peel pears, cut in half lengthways
and remove core. Beat egg, sugar, salt,
spices, lemon rind and sour cream together
in a food processor or blender.

*Topping:* Mix all ingredients together in
either a food processor or blender until
mixture resembles coarse breadcrumbs.

*To finish tart:* Roll pastry out thinly and
line a 23 cm (9 inch) flan tin. Trim and
decorate edge and prick base. Place pears
neatly into pastry case, narrow tops
towards the centre. Pour egg and sour
cream mixture over and sprinkle with
topping. Bake in the centre of a hot oven
at 200°C (400°F) for 25 minutes or until
filling is set. Cool on a wire cooling tray.
Serve tart warm with whipped cream.

# Lemon Chess Pie

*Serves 6-8.*

155 g (1 quantity) lard pastry (see page
14)

*Filling:*
4 x 60 g eggs
250 g (1 cup) castor sugar
60 ml (¼ cup) cream
60 ml (¼ cup) lemon juice
60 g (2 tablespoons) butter, melted and
cooled
4 tablespoons finely crushed coconut
macaroons
1 tablespoon finely grated lemon rind

Make pastry according to recipe and chill
well.

*Filling:* Place eggs in Kenwood bowl and
beat at maximum speed for 60 seconds or
until light and fluffy. Gradually add sugar,
beating continuously at maximum speed
until mixture is thick (approx. 5-6 minutes).
Add remaining ingredients and mix for a
few seconds, until well combined.

*To finish pie:* Roll pastry out thinly and line a 23 cm (9 inch) flan tin or pie plate. Prick base and chill pastry case for 30 minutes. Carefully spoon filling into prepared pastry case, standing on a baking tray. Bake in the centre of a very hot oven at 230°C (430°F) for 5 minutes, reduce temperature to moderately hot, 190°C (375°F), and bake for a further 20-25 minutes, or until filling is set. Transfer pie to a wire cooling tray to cool. Serve warm or cold with whipped cream.

# Lemon and Orange Tart

*Serves 8.*

185 g (¾ quantity) rich short crust pastry or pâte sucrée (see pages 12, 13)

*Filling:*
**4 x 60 g eggs**
**185 g (¾ cup) sugar**
**165 ml (⅔ cup) lemon juice**
**125 ml (½ cup) orange juice**
**grated rind of 2 lemons**
**60 g (2 tablespoons) butter**
**60 ml (¼ cup) cream**

*Topping:*
**1 lemon**
**1 tablespoon castor sugar**

Make pastry according to recipe and chill well.

*Filling:* Place eggs, sugar, lemon juice, orange juice and lemon rind in bowl of Kenwood mixer and whisk at maximum speed for 30 seconds. In a double-boiler, melt butter with cream, add egg mixture and cook over simmering water, stirring constantly, until the mixture coats the back of a metal spoon and thickens. Do not let it boil. Leave to cool, covered with a round of buttered waxed paper.

*To finish tart:* Roll pastry dough out thinly and line a 23 cm (9 inch) flan tin. Prick base and bake 'blind' in a hot oven at 200°C (400°F) for 10 minutes, then remove 'blind' filling and paper and bake for a further 10-15 minutes, until it is lightly coloured. Remove tart case from tin carefully and cool on a wire cooling tray. Pour the custard into the tart case and bake towards the top of a moderately hot oven at 190°C (375°F) for 20 minutes.

*Topping:* Using a sharp, serrated knife, peel and segment the lemon, making sure to remove all membrane, and arrange segments around top of tart. Cover the pastry edge with a strip of foil. Sprinkle castor sugar over tart and glaze top by placing under a preheated grill for 1 minute. Remove the foil and serve the tart warm with whipped cream.

# Normandy Apple Tart

*Serves 6.*

250 g (1 quantity) pâte sucrée or 185 g (1 quantity) one-stage short crust pastry (see pages 12, 13)

*Filling:*
**4 large green cooking apples**
**2 tablespoons sugar**
**2 tablespoons cold water**
**2 red apples**
**juice of 2 lemons**
**30 g (1 tablespoon) butter, melted**
**3 tablespoons apricot jam**

Make pastry according to recipe and chill well.

*Filling:* Peel, core and slice cooking apples into a heavy-based pan. Add sugar and water, cover and stew gently until tender and thick. Cool, then mix apples to a purée in an electric blender or food processor. Core and slice red apples very thinly and dip into lemon juice.

*To finish tart:* Roll pastry out on a lightly floured board to a round and line a 20 or 23 cm (8 or 9 inch) flan tin. Prick base of pastry case, chill for 30 minutes, then bake 'blind' towards the top of a hot oven at 220°C (425°F) for 10-15 minutes or until base is firm. Spread apple purée in flan case and cover neatly with circles of overlapping slices of red apple. Brush apples with melted butter and return to oven for a further 15-20 minutes or until apple is golden. Remove flan from oven and cool on a wire cooling tray for 5-10 minutes, then remove side and base of flan tin when pastry is firm. Warm the apricot jam and brush on top of flan, coating apples completely. Serve cold with whipped cream.

# Plum and Brandy Tart

*Serves 6.*

**185 g (¾ quantity) rich short crust pastry
or pâte sucrée (see pages 12, 13)**

*Filling:*
**1 kg (2 lb) ripe plums**
**30 g (¼ cup) ground almonds**
**4 tablespoons vanilla sugar**
**2 x 60 g eggs**
**5 tablespoons cream**
**4 tablespoons brandy**
**1 tablespoon orange flower water**
**30 g (1 tablespoon) butter, melted**

Prepare pastry according to recipe and
chill well.

*Filling:* Cut plums in half and remove
stones. Mix ground almonds, vanilla sugar,
eggs, cream, brandy and orange flower
water together in the Kenwood mixer with
the whisk. Add melted butter and mix well.

*To finish tart:* Roll pastry out thinly and
line a 23 cm (9 inch) flan tin. Trim and
decorate edge. Prick base of pastry case.
Arrange plums, overlapping, in circles in
the pastry case, starting round the edge
and finishing in the centre. Pour the egg
mixture over the plums. Bake towards the
top of a hot oven at 220°C (425°F) for 25
minutes or until fruit is cooked and filling is
set. Serve warm or cold with whipped
cream.

**Variation:** Apricot and Brandy Tart—substitute fresh apricots for plums.

# Prune Flan

*Serves 6.*

**185 g (¾ quantity) rich short crust pastry
or pâte sucrée (see pages 12, 13)**

*Filling:*
**375 g (1¾ cups)dessert prunes**
**125 ml (½ cup) red wine**
**3 tablespoons redcurrant jelly**
**60 g (½ cup) ground almonds**
**2 tablespoons castor sugar**
**½ egg white**
**2 tablespoons custard powder**
**2 teaspoons sugar**
**125 ml (½ cup) milk**
**200 ml (1 small jar) cream**

Make pastry according to recipe and chill
well.

*Filling:* Place prunes and red wine in a pan,
cover tightly and simmer until tender,
about 15-20 minutes. Remove prunes from
wine, using a slotted spoon. Add redcurrant jelly to wine and dissolve over a low
heat, then strain to make a glaze. Remove
stones from prunes neatly. Mix ground
almonds and castor sugar together. Whisk
egg white until stiff, then fold sufficient into
the ground almond mixture to bind to a
smooth paste. Place a roll of almond paste
neatly into each prune. Blend custard
powder and 2 teaspoons sugar with the
milk in a saucepan until smooth, then bring
to the boil, stirring continuously. Leave to
cool. Whip cream and fold into the cold
custard.

*To finish flan:* Roll pastry out thinly and
line a 20 cm (8 inch) flan tin. Bake 'blind'
as for Apricot and Almond Flan (see page
75). Pour custard cream into the baked
pastry case and spread smooth. Arrange
almond stuffed prunes attractively on top
of custard and cover neatly with the redcurrant glaze. Allow to set before serving.
Serve with whipped cream.

# Rhubarb Flan

*Serves 6.*

**250 g (1 quantity) pâte sucrée (see page
13)**

*Filling:*
**1 kg (2 lb) rhubarb**
**500 g (2 cups) sugar**
**250 ml (1 cup) water**
**1 punnet strawberries**

*Glaze:*
**125 ml (½ cup) rhubarb syrup**
**1 tablespoon brandy**
**2 teaspoons arrowroot**

Make pastry according to recipe and chill
well.

*Filling:* Wash and trim rhubarb, cut into 3
cm (1½ inch) lengths and measure 6 cups.
In a large heavy-based pan or boiler, combine sugar and water and stir over a low
heat until sugar is dissolved, then bring to
the boil. Increase heat to medium and simmer syrup for 5 minutes. Add half the rhubarb and simmer for 3-6 minutes, removing

pieces when they are just tender, making sure rhubarb retains its shape. Carefully transfer rhubarb to a shallow dish, using a slotted spoon. Simmer remaining rhubarb in syrup in the same way. Transfer to dish when just tender, pour syrup over and allow mixture to cool

*To finish flan:* On a lightly floured board, roll out pastry to a round and line a 23 cm (9 inch) flan tin. Bake pastry 'blind' towards the top of a hot oven at 200°C (400°F) for 15 minutes. Carefully remove 'blind' filling and paper and bake pastry for a further 15 minutes, or until lightly coloured. Transfer to a wire cooling tray and allow to cool. As near to serving time as possible, transfer rhubarb with a slotted spoon to cold pastry case, arranging it in overlapping rows. Arrange hulled and halved strawberries around the edge.

*Glaze:* Measure 125 ml (½ cup) of rhubarb syrup and place in a saucepan. Add brandy. In a small bowl, blend arrowroot with a little of the measured syrup until smooth then pour into the saucepan. Bring to the boil over a medium heat, stirring continuously, simmer for 1 minute, then allow to cool. Spoon glaze over rhubarb and strawberries and chill in refrigerator until glaze is set before serving. Serve with whipped cream.

# Strawberry Flan

*Serves 6.*

**185 g (¾ quantity) rich short crust pastry or pâte sucrée (see pages 12, 13)**

***Filling:***
**2-3 punnets strawberries, depending on size of berries**
**300 ml (1 jar/carton) cream**
**6 tablespoons redcurrant jelly**
**2 teaspoons arrowroot or cornflour**
**1 tablespoon cold water**
**approx. 3 tablespoons orange juice**

Prepare pastry according to recipe and chill well.

*Filling:* Hull strawberries and pick over to make sure they are clean. Whip cream until thick. Heat redcurrant jelly in a saucepan until melted and smooth. Blend cornflour with cold water until smooth. Stir into redcurrant jelly and bring to the boil, stirring continuously until mixture is thick, clear

and smooth. Stir in sufficient orange juice to give a smooth consistency.

*To finish flan:* Roll pastry out thinly and line a 23 cm (9 inch) flan tin. Bake 'blind' as for Apricot and Almond Flan (see page 75) then leave to cool. Spread cream evenly over the bottom of the flan case. Arrange strawberries attractively on top of cream, then spread or brush redcurrant glaze over. Serve flan cold.

**Variation:** Strawberry and Grape Flan— grapes may be substituted for some of the strawberries. Raspberry Flan—substitute fresh raspberries for strawberries.

# Fruit Tartlets

*Makes 12.*

**185 g (¾ quantity) rich short crust pastry or pâte sucrée (see pages 12, 13)**

***Filling:***
**selection of fresh or canned fruit, e.g., strawberries, raspberries, Chinese gooseberries, cherries, canned apricot halves or mandarin oranges**
**250 ml (1 cup) redcurrant jelly**

Make pastry according to recipe and chill well.

*Filling:* Prepare fruit accordingly. Hull and clean strawberries, slice large berries. Pick raspberries over. Peel Chinese gooseberries and slice thickly. Stone cherries. Drain canned fruit well.

*To finish tartlets:* Roll pastry out thinly on a lightly floured board, cut into rounds with a floured pastry cutter and line 12 x 8 cm (3 inch) tartlet tins. Press pastry neatly into tins and trim off excess by rolling lightly over top of tins with a rolling pin. Prick bottom of pastry cases with a fork, place tins on a baking tray and bake 'blind' at the top of a hot oven at 200°C (400°F) for 10-15 minutes or until cooked. Cool pastry cases in tins on a wire cooling tray for a few minutes, then remove from tins and cool completely. Arrange fruit neatly in tartlet cases. Heat redcurrant jelly in a saucepan until warm and runny, then brush jelly generously over the fruit until completely covered. Allow to cool and set. Serve for a special afternoon tea or at a coffee party or as a dessert with whipped cream.

# Treacle Tart

*Serves 6.*

**185 g (1 quantity) sweet short crust pastry
    (see page 11)**

*Filling:*
**8 tablespoons golden syrup
6 tablespoons fresh white breadcrumbs
finely grated rind of 1 lemon
1 tablespoon lemon juice**

Prepare pastry according to recipe and chill well.

*Filling:* Mix all ingredients together.

*To finish tart:* Roll pastry out to a round and line a 20 cm (8 inch) ovenproof plate. Trim off excess. Spread filling over to within 2.5 cm (1 inch) of edge. Roll remaining scraps of pastry out and cut into thin strips. Twist strips and place in a lattice over the filling, sealing ends with water. Bake towards the top of a hot oven at 220°C (425°F) for 20-30 minutes or until pastry is cooked. Serve warm with custard or cream.

**Note:** Dip measuring spoon into very hot water before measuring golden syrup.

**Variation:** Try adding 1 grated apple to the treacle filling.

# Walnut Tart

*Serves 6-8.*

**185 g (1 quantity) pâte sucrée (see page
    13)**

*Filling:*
**125 g (½ cup) sugar
3 tablespoons water
pinch of cream of tartar
60 g (1 cup) coarsely chopped walnuts
125 ml (½ cup) honey
250 ml (1 cup) cream
2 x 60 g eggs, lightly beaten**

Make pastry according to recipe and chill well.

*Filling:* Place sugar, water and cream of tartar in a heavy-based saucepan. Bring slowly to the boil over a low heat, stirring and washing down any sugar crystals clinging to sides of pan with a brush dipped in cold water, until sugar is dissolved.

Increase heat to medium and cook syrup until it is a deep caramel colour. Add chopped walnuts (prepared in a blender or food processor), honey and cream, and cook over a high heat for 2-3 minutes or until slightly thickened. Reduce heat to low, stir in eggs and cook gently for 2 minutes.

*To finish tart:* Roll pastry out to a thin round and line a 23 cm (9 inch) flan tin. Bake 'blind' towards the top of a hot oven at 200°C (400°F) for 10 minutes, remove baking beans and paper ('blind' filling) and bake in a moderately hot oven at 190°C (375°F) for a further 10-15 minutes or until pastry is light golden and cooked. Place on a wire cooling tray and allow to cool. Pour mixture into pastry case and leave to stand at room temperature for 1 hour. Transfer Walnut Tart to refrigerator and chill for a further 1-2 hours. Allow tart to come back to room temperature before serving.

# Currant Tartlets

*Makes 12.*

**185 g (¾ quantity) rich short crust pastry
    or pâte sucrée (see pages 12, 13)**

*Filling:*
**185 g (6 oz) packaged cream cheese
4 tablespoons cream
1 tablespoon castor sugar
250 g (approx. 1 punnet) blackcurrants or
    redcurrants
250 ml (1 cup) redcurrant jelly**

Make pastry according to recipe and chill well.

*Filling:* Mix cream cheese with cream and sugar in either a blender or food processor until smooth. Top and tail currants.

*To finish tartlets:* Roll dough out thinly and line 12 x 8 cm (3 inch) tartlet cases (as for Fruit Tartlets, page 83). Prick bottom of pastry cases, place tins on a baking tray, and bake 'blind' at the top of a hot oven at 200°C (400°F) for 10-15 minutes or until cooked. Cool on a wire cooling tray. Spread cream cheese filling neatly in the cold tartlet cases. Place currants on top of cream cheese covering neatly. Heat redcurrant jelly gently in a saucepan until clear and runny. Spoon warm redcurrant jelly over currants and leave to set. Serve cold as a dessert or with coffee.

# Filbert Tarts

*Makes 12.*

*Pastry:*
155 g (1¼ cups) plain flour
pinch of salt
90 g (3 tablespoons) butter
45 g (1½ tablespoons) castor sugar
30 g (¼ cup) finely chopped hazelnuts
½ beaten egg

*Filling:*
60 g (2 tablespoons) butter
60 g (¼ cup) sugar
1 egg, beaten
1 teaspoon coffee essence
1 teaspoon honey
45 g (4 tablespoons) hazelnuts, finely
   chopped
30 g (¼ cup) cake or biscuit crumbs
1 tablespoon plain flour
1 tablespoon milk
raspberry jam

*Coffee Icing:*
90 g (3 tablespoons) soft butter or
   margarine
250 g (2 cups) icing sugar, sifted
1 tablespoon coffee essence
crystallized mimosa or flower petals for
   decoration

*Pastry:* Sift flour and salt into the Kenwood bowl. Cut butter into small pieces, then mix in as for Short Crust Pastry (see page 11). Add sugar and hazelnuts, then mix to a stiff dough with beaten egg. Wrap dough in greaseproof paper and chill in refrigerator for at least 30 minutes.

*Filling:* Cream butter and sugar together in a food processor until light and fluffy. Add remaining ingredients except raspberry jam and mix well to a smooth consistency.

*To finish tartlets:* Roll pastry out thinly on a lightly floured board and line a tray of 12 tartlet tins. Place ½ teaspoon raspberry jam in each tartlet case and cover neatly with a heaped teaspoon of filling. Bake tartlets at the top of a hot oven at 200°C (400°F) for 15-20 minutes, until cooked. Cool on a wire cooling tray.

*Coffee icing:* Place all ingredients in a bowl and mix with an electric mixer until soft and fluffy, like whipped cream. Pipe small rosettes of coffee icing on top of tartlets and decorate with crystallized mimosa.

**Note:** Small jars of crystallized mimosa or flower petals are available at leading delicatessens.

# Swedish Mazarin Tarts

*Makes 12.*

185 g (¾ quantity) rich short crust pastry
   (see page 12)

*Filling:*
250 g (8 oz) packet marzipan or almond
   paste
2 tablespoons sugar
2 tablespoons plain flour
2 x 60 g eggs
1 egg white
¼ teaspoon almond essence

*Icing:*
125 g (1 cup) pure icing sugar
2 tablespoons milk

Make pastry according to recipe and chill well.

*Filling:* Break almond paste into small pieces into a food processor or the bowl of the Kenwood mixer, blend smoothly with sugar and flour. Add eggs and egg white separately and mix until blended. Stir in almond essence.

*To finish tarts:* Roll pastry out thinly and line a tray of 12 tartlet tins. Prick the base of each tartlet case. Spoon an equal quantity of filling into each tartlet case. Bake towards the top of a moderately slow oven at 160°C (325°F) for 30 minutes or until pastries are richly browned on top. Allow tarts to cool about 5 minutes in the tartlet tins before removing and transferring to a wire cooling tray.

*Icing:* Blend sifted icing sugar smoothly with milk. Spoon equal quantities of icing onto each cooled mazarin and spread to coat top evenly. Serve at once with coffee or tea or store in an airtight container for up to two days at room temperature. Freeze for longer storage.

# CUSTARD PIES

Think of slap-stick comedy and you immediately think of custard pies, but it makes me almost cry to think of all those good ingredients and time and care going to waste.

A custard pie is one of the lightest, most delicate and nourishing pies possible. Ideal for young children, old people, invalids and people with digestive problems as well as delicious to accompany a quiet cup of tea.

The custard pie has now become international and each nation has added its individual touch, with coconuts and rum, limes, pecans and pumpkin. They are still all delicious.

# Tip

Brush the pastry case with lightly whisked egg white to form a seal before placing custard filling in.

# Butterscotch Pie

*Serves 6.*

**185 g (¾ quantity) rich short crust pastry or pâte sucrée (see pages 12, 13)**

*Filling:*
**1 tablespoon custard powder**
**250 ml (1 cup) evaporated milk**
**90 g (½ cup) brown sugar**
**1 tablespoon honey**
**1 teaspoon vanilla essence**
**1 teaspoon vinegar**
**60 g (½ cup) chopped dates**
**200 ml (1 small jar) cream for decoration**

Prepare pastry according to recipe and chill well.

*Filling:* Blend custard powder with 3 tablespoons of the measured milk in a saucepan. Add remaining milk, then stir in sugar, honey, vanilla and vinegar. Bring to the boil, stirring continuously.

*To finish pie:* Roll pastry out thinly and line a 20 or 23 cm (8 or 9 inch) flan tin. Bake 'blind', then cool. Sprinkle dates over the bottom of the pastry case. Pour filling into the pastry case and chill in refrigerator until firm. Whip cream and pipe around the edge of the pie. Serve cold.

# Coconut Rum Tart

*Serves 6.*

**185 g (¾ quantity) rich short crust pastry or pâte sucrée (see pages 12, 13)**

*Filling:*
**200 g (approx. 2 cups) grated fresh coconut**
**1 x 60 g egg**
**2 egg yolks**
**90 g (3 tablespoons) castor sugar**
**90 g (3 tablespoons) butter, melted**
**3 tablespoons dark rum**

Make pastry according to recipe and chill well.

*Filling:* Remove fresh coconut from shell, cut flesh into chunky pieces and trim off brown skin. Place coconut chunks in either a blender or a food processor and mix until grated. Spread grated coconut on a baking tray and place in a moderate oven at 180°C (350°F) until golden. Place egg, egg yolks and sugar in the Kenwood bowl and whisk until thick and light in colour. The mixture should be stiff enough to support its own trail. Stir in the melted butter and rum, then fold in the coconut.

*To finish tart:* Roll pastry out thinly on a lightly floured board and line a 23 cm (9 inch) flan tin. Prick base well and chill for 20 minutes. Pour filling into pastry case and bake towards the top of a moderate oven at 180°C (350°F) for 30 minutes or until cooked. Serve cold with whipped cream.

# Egg Nog Pie

*Serves 8.*

**250 g (1 quantity) rich short crust pastry (see page 12)**

**Filling:**
**300 ml (1¼ cups) milk**
**125 g (½ cup) castor sugar**
**4 x 60 g eggs, separated**
**1 tablespoon gelatine**
**60 ml (¼ cup) cold water**
**150 ml (½ jar/carton) cream**
**1 tablespoon brandy**
**1 tablespoon castor sugar**
**extra 150 ml (½ jar/carton) cream, whipped for decoration**
**60 g (2 oz) dark cooking chocolate, grated**

Make pastry according to recipe and chill well.

*Filling:* Heat milk to lukewarm. Lightly beat together sugar and egg in the bowl of the Kenwood mixer with a whisk at speed 3 for 30 seconds. Add warm milk and whisk at speed 2 for 30 seconds. Pour mixture into the top of a double-boiler and cook over gently bubbling water, stirring continuously, until custard coats the back of a metal spoon. Pour thickened custard into a bowl and leave to cool with a piece of wet waxed paper over the top to prevent a skin forming. Soak gelatine in ¼ cup cold water, then stand in a hot-water bath until dissolved. Gradually add lukewarm gelatine to lukewarm custard and stir well, then leave to partially set. Whip cream and fold through the custard together with the brandy. Place egg whites in the Kenwood bowl and whisk at maximum speed for 2 minutes or until stiff, gradually add sugar and continue whisking to form a stiff

meringue. Gently fold meringue into custard.

*To finish pie:* Roll pastry out thinly and line a lightly greased round 23 cm (9 inch) pie plate. Trim and decorate edge and prick base. Place on a baking tray and bake 'blind' towards the top of a moderately hot oven at 190°C (375°F) for 10 minutes, then remove 'blind' filling and bake for a further 10-15 minutes or until lightly browned. Cool by standing pie plate on a wire cooling tray. Pour filling into cold pastry case and leave to set. Serve cold, decorated with rosettes of whipped cream and grated chocolate or chocolate curls.

# English Custard Tart

*Serves 6-8.*

**185 g (¾ quantity) rich short crust pastry (see page 12)**
**egg white for sealing**

**Filling:**
**3 x 60 g eggs**
**1 tablespoon castor sugar**
**300 ml (1¼ cups) milk**
**¼ teaspoon vanilla essence**
**freshly grated nutmeg**

Make pastry according to recipe and chill well.

*Filling:* Break eggs into the bowl of the Kenwood mixer and beat with the whisk until egg runs smoothly through the wires of the whisk. Add sugar, milk and vanilla essence and stir well.

*To finish tart:* Roll pastry out thinly and line a deep 20 cm (8 inch) flan tin. Press base of pastry case down firmly, then place tin on a baking tray and bake 'blind' in a hot oven at 200°C (400°F) for 10-15 minutes, until set in shape. Brush bottom of pastry case with lightly whisked egg white, then strain filling into pastry case. Sprinkle grated nutmeg on top. Place tart in the top of the oven at 200°C (400°F) for 7 minutes, then bake at moderate at 180°C (350°F) for a further 7-12 minutes or until custard is set. Allow custard to cool before removing from flan tin. Serve cold as a dessert or with a cup of tea.

# Key Lime Pie

*Serves 6-8.*

**155 g (1 quantity) lard pastry (see page 14)**

**Filling:**
**5 x 60 g egg yolks**
**1 x 450 g can condensed milk**
**125 ml (½ cup) lime *or* lemon juice**
**3 x 60 g egg whites**
**300 ml (1 jar/carton) thickened cream,**
**  whipped for decoration**

Make pastry according to instructions and chill well.

*Filling:* Beat egg yolks in the bowl of the Kenwood mixer with a wire whisk until thick, about 3 minutes. Slowly beat in the condensed milk and lime juice. Whisk egg whites at maximum speed until stiff and fold into the lime mixture with a spatula.

*To finish pie:* Roll pastry out thinly and line a 23 cm (9 inch) pie plate or a 23 cm (9 inch) flan tin. Prick base well. Bake pastry case 'blind' at the top of a hot oven at 200°C (400°F) for 10 minutes, remove 'blind' filling and paper and bake for a further 10 minutes at moderate, at 180°C (350°F). Cool on a wire cooling tray. Pour filling into baked pastry case and bake in the middle of a moderately slow oven at 160-180°C (325-350°F) for 20-30 minutes or until filling is firm. Serve warm or cold, decorated with whipped cream.

# Milk Tart

*Serves 6-8.*

**250 g (1 quantity) puff, rough puff or flaky**
**  pastry (see pages 15, 16)**

**Filling:**
**500 ml (2 cups) milk**
**1 stick of cinnamon**
**1 tablespoon cornflour**
**2 tablespoons sugar**
**½ teaspoon salt**
**30 g (1 tablespoon) butter or margarine**
**3 x 60 g eggs**
**1 teaspoon sugar and 1 teaspoon ground**
**  cinnamon for sprinkling**

Make pastry according to recipe and chill well.

*Filling:* Infuse milk and cinnamon stick in the top of a double-boiler for 30 minutes. Place cornflour, sugar and salt into a mixing bowl. Remove cinnamon stick and stir hot milk into cornflour mixture. Pour into a saucepan and bring to the boil, stirring continuously. Reduce heat and simmer, covered, for 15 minutes. Remove from heat and stir in butter. Cool, then mix in well beaten eggs.

*To finish tart:* Roll pastry out to a thin round and line a 23 cm (9 inch) tart plate. Place filling in pastry case and bake in the middle of a hot oven at 200°C (400°F) for 20 minutes, then reduce temperature to moderately hot, 190°C (375°F), and bake for a further 10 minutes or until filling is set. Serve hot or warm sprinkled with sugar and ground cinnamon.

# Pecan Pie

*Serves 8.*

**155 g (1 quantity) lard pastry (see page 14)**

**Filling:**
**4 x 60 g eggs**
**475 ml (approx. 2 cups) golden syrup**
**30 g (1 tablespoon) butter, melted**
**1 teaspoon vanilla essence**
**185 g (1½ cups) pecan nuts**

Make pastry according to recipe and chill well.

*Filling:* Beat eggs in the bowl of the Kenwood mixer. Pour golden syrup into beaten eggs and beat well. Beat in melted butter and vanilla. Stir in pecan nuts.

*To finish pie:* Roll pastry out thinly and line a 23 cm (9 inch) pie plate. Trim and decorate edge, then place pie plate on a baking tray and bake 'blind' towards the top of a hot oven at 220°C (425°F) for 12-15 minutes, until pastry is set in shape. Remove 'blind' filling and paper and bake for a further 5 minutes. Carefully pour filling into the pastry case and bake in a hot oven at 220°C (425°F) for 30-35 minutes or until filling is firm. Serve either warm or cold with whipped cream.

# Pumpkin Pie

*Serves 8.*

**250 g (1 quantity) American pastry (see page 14)**

*Filling:*
**125 g (⅔ cup) soft brown sugar**
**pinch of salt**
**1 teaspoon ground cinnamon**
**½ teaspoon ground ginger**
**¼ teaspoon ground nutmeg**
**2 x 60 g eggs**
**150 ml (½ jar/carton) cream or evaporated milk**
**250 g (1 cup) mashed cooked pumpkin**

*Topping:*
**200 ml (1 small jar) thickened cream**
**1 teaspoon castor sugar**
**¼ teaspoon grated nutmeg**
**60 g (½ cup) walnuts, chopped**

Make pastry according to recipe and chill well.

*Filling:* Mix sugar, salt and spices together in a small bowl. Beat eggs in a second bowl until smooth, then stir in the cream and milk. Gently fold in mashed pumpkin. Stir sugar and spices into pumpkin mixture.

*To finish pie:* Roll out pastry on a lightly floured board to a round and line a 23 cm (9 inch) pie plate. Trim edge with a sharp knife and prick base with a fork. Decorate edge by fluting pastry with the thumb and forefingers. Refrigerate pastry case for 20 minutes. Pour filling into pastry case, then place pie plate on a baking tray and bake in a moderate oven at 180°C (350°F) for 1 hour or until pastry is cooked and filling is set. Stand pie plate on a wire cooling tray to cool.

*Topping:* Whip cream until stiff and fold in castor sugar and grated nutmeg. Spread cream over pumpkin filling and sprinkle with walnuts. Serve cold as a dessert.

# Raisin Custard Tart

*Serves 6.*

**185 g (1 quantity) sweet short crust pastry (see page 11)**

*Filling:*
**3 x 60 g eggs**
**60 g (¼ cup) castor sugar**
**¼ teaspoon salt**
**½ teaspoon vanilla essence**
**90 g (½ cup) seedless raisins**
**375 ml (1½ cups) milk**
**freshly grated or ground nutmeg**

Make pastry according to recipe and chill well.

*Filling:* Place eggs, sugar, salt and vanilla essence in the Kenwood mixer bowl and whisk on speed 5 for 30 seconds.

*To finish tart:* Roll pastry out thinly and line a deep 20 cm (8 inch) flan tin. Chill in refrigerator for 20 minutes. Place flan tin on a baking tray and sprinkle raisins over the bottom. Heat milk almost to boiling point, then slowly stir into egg mixture. Mix well and strain at once into the pastry case and sprinkle with freshly ground nutmeg. Bake tart just above the centre of a very hot oven at 230°C (450°F) for 5 minutes, then reduce temperature to hot, 220°C (425°F), for 20-25 minutes, or until a knife inserted in the centre comes out clean. Cool on a wire cooling tray for 5 minutes before removing sides of flan tin. Serve warm or chilled with whipped cream.

# MERINGUE PIES

Meringue pies always look mouth-watering and usually taste as good as they look. They are invariably sweet filled pies topped with a soft-textured golden meringue which is easy to cut when serving and is light and delicate to eat. The Pavlova Pie is an exception as it is all meringue and is topped with whipped cream or yoghurt and fruit.

Successful meringue making requires a large, scrupulously clean bowl and continuously fast whisking which is all made much easier with the use of your powerful Kenwood mixer.

## Tip

Make sure the Kenwood bowl is scrupulously clean before placing egg white in it —the tiniest speck of grease, detergent or egg yolk will prevent the egg from whisking stiffly.

# Apple Amber

*Serves 4-6.*

**125 g (½ quantity) short crust pastry (see page 11)**

*Filling:*
**4 cooking apples**
**2 tablespoons sugar**
**rind and juice of 1 lemon**
**30 g (1 tablespoon) butter**
**2 x 60 g egg yolks**

*Meringue:*
**2 x 60 g egg whites**
**4 tablespoons castor sugar**

Prepare pastry according to recipe and chill well.

*Filling:* Peel, core and slice apples. Place in a saucepan with 2 tablespoons sugar and rind and juice of lemon and stew gently, tightly covered, for 10-15 minutes or until apples have fallen to a 'mush'. Cool, then mix to a purée in a blender or food processor. Add butter and egg yolks to purée, and mix until evenly combined.

*To finish amber:* Roll out pastry thinly to an oval and line a 1 litre (4 cup) oval pie dish. Trim, flake and decorate edge. Pour apple filling into pastry pie case and bake in the middle of a hot oven at 220°C (425°F) for 15 minutes or until pastry is golden brown and cooked.

*Meringue:* Whisk egg whites in Kenwood mixer at maximum speed until stiff. Add castor sugar slowly and continuously, whisking the egg whites at top speed until a stiff shiny meringue forms. Place meringue on top of apple filling and swirl into a windswept pattern with a plastic spatula. Return apple amber to a moderate oven at 180°C (350°F) and cook for a further 15-20 minutes or until meringue is golden. Serve warm with cream or egg custard.

# Butterscotch Tart

*Serves 6.*

**185 g (¾ quantity) rich short crust pastry or pâte sucrée (see pages 12, 13)**

**Filling:**
**125 g (⅔ cup) brown sugar**
**pinch of salt**
**4 tablespoons plain flour**
**500 ml (2 cups) milk**
**2 x 60 g egg yolks, lightly beaten**
**60 g (2 tablespoons) butter**
**1 teaspoon vanilla essence**

**Meringue:**
**2 x 60 g egg whites**
**4 tablespoons castor sugar**

Make pastry according to recipe and chill well.

*Filling:* Place brown sugar, salt and flour in bowl and blend lightly with the K beater on minimum speed. Add a little milk, increase speed to 2 and beat for 60 seconds. Add remaining milk on speed 1 and blend for a further 30 seconds. Transfer mixture to a heavy-based saucepan and bring to the boil over a medium heat, stirring continuously. Simmer for 2 minutes. Remove from heat, add egg yolks, butter and vanilla and stir in thoroughly.

*To finish tart :*Roll pastry out thinly and line a 23 cm (9 inch) flan tin and bake 'blind' for 15 minutes. Remove 'blind' filling and cool on a wire cooling tray. Pour butterscotch filling into cooled pastry case and allow to stand while making meringue.

*Meringue:* Place egg whites in the clean dry bowl of the Kenwood mixer and, using whisk, whisk egg whites on maximum speed for 1 minute 45 seconds, then gradually add sugar, still at maximum speed, and continue to whisk until all sugar is incorporated. Spread meringue over butterscotch filling, sealing at the edge of the tart. Place in a slow oven at 160°C (325°F) for 15-20 minutes or until meringue is golden. Serve warm or cold.

# Frangipani Pie

*Serves 6-8.*

**185 g (¾ quantity) rich short crust pastry**
  **or pâte sucrée (see pages 12, 13)**

**Filling:**
**1st layer:**
**185 ml (¾ cup) evaporated milk**
**125 ml (½ cup) water**
**60 g (¼ cup) sugar**
**pinch of salt**

**2 tablespoons cornflour**
**90 g (1 cup) desiccated coconut**
**30 g (1 tablespoon) butter**
**1 teaspoon vanilla essence**

**2nd layer:**
**450 g can crushed pineapple**
**2 tablespoons cornflour**
**60 ml (¼ cup) water**
**2 x 60 g egg yolks**

**Meringue:**
**2 x 60 g egg whites**
**4 tablespoons castor sugar**

Prepare pastry according to recipe and chill well.

*Filling: 1st layer:* Place evaporated milk, half the water, sugar and salt in a heavy-based saucepan and stir over a low heat until mixture comes to the boil and sugar has dissolved. Blend remaining water and cornflour together to a smooth paste. Add to milk mixture, stirring until mixture thickens. Remove from heat, stir in coconut, butter and vanilla, then allow to cool slightly.

*2nd layer:* Place pineapple and juice in a heavy-based saucepan and bring to the boil. Blend cornflour, water and egg yolks to a smooth paste. Add to pineapple and stir over a low heat until thick. Allow to cool slightly.

*To finish pie:* Roll pastry out on a lightly floured board to a round and line a deep 20 cm (8 inch) flan tin. Bake 'blind', then cool on a wire cooling tray. Place 1st layer of filling in pastry case and top with 2nd layer.

*Meringue:* In the clean, polished bowl of the Kenwood mixer, whisk egg whites at maximum speed until stiff, then gradually add sugar, whisking continuously at top speed. Spoon meringue on top of pie and swirl with a round-bladed knife to give a windswept appearance. Bake in a moderate oven at 180°C (350°F) for 15 minutes or until golden. Serve warm or cold.

# Lemon Meringue Pie

*Serves 6.*

**185 g (¾ quantity) rich short crust pastry
(see page 12)**

*Filling:*
**30 g (1 tablespoon) soft butter or
margarine
60 g (4 tablespoons) cornflour
300 ml (1¼ cups) water
finely grated rind and juice of 1 large or
2 small lemons
125 g (½ cup) castor sugar
2 x 60 g egg yolks**

*Meringue:*
**2 x 60 g egg whites
4 tablespoons castor sugar**

Make pastry as directed in recipe and chill
well.

*Filling:* Place all ingredients, except egg
yolks, in a saucepan. Bring to the boil over
a medium heat, whisking continuously with
a wire balloon-shaped whisk, or beating
gently with a wooden spoon. Reduce heat
and continue beating for 1-2 minutes. Cool,
then beat in egg yolks.

*To finish pie:* Roll pastry out thinly and line
a deep 20 cm (8 inch) flan tin. Prick bottom
of flan lightly, then line with greaseproof
paper and baking beans. Bake towards the
top of a hot oven at 220°C (425°F) for 15
minutes, remove 'blind' filling and return
to oven at moderately hot, 190°C (375°F),
for a further 15 minutes. Cool on a wire
cooling tray. Pour filling into cool pastry
flan case.

*Meringue:* Place egg whites in a clean
Kenwood mixing bowl and whisk at maximum speed until stiff. Whisk in half castor
sugar gradually and continuously, whisking
at maximum speed until stiff. Fold in remaining sugar gently with a metal spoon.
Place meringue gently on top of lemon
filling and spread neatly to edge of flan
case, using a plastic spatula, and swirl the
top. Bake in the middle of a moderately
slow oven at 160°C (325°F) for 15-20
minutes, or until meringue is golden. This
gives a soft-cooked meringue, typical of a
lemon meringue pie. If you prefer a crisper,
drier meringue, place in a slow oven at
100°C (200°F) for 1-1½ hours. Serve warm
or cold.

# Yoghurt Pavlova

*Serves 6-8.*

*Meringue:*
**4 x 60 g egg whites
250 g (1 cup) castor sugar
1 teaspoon vinegar
1 teaspoon vanilla essence
1 tablespoon cornflour**

*Topping:*
**1 x 200 g carton apricot yoghurt
2 passionfruit**

*Meringue:* Whisk egg whites in clean
polished bowl of Kenwood mixer at maximum speed until stiff. Add sugar continuously, a teaspoonful at a time, whisking
continuously at maximum speed, then stop
mixer. Fold vinegar, vanilla and cornflour
gently into meringue with a plastic spatula.
Spread mixture in a 20 cm (8 inch) circle
on a baking tray, previously lined with rice
paper or greaseproof paper and well oiled.
Place pavlova in a cool oven at 120°C
(250°F) for 2 hours or until crisp and dry.
Allow to cool slightly, but loosen from
paper, then cool on a wire cooling tray.

*To finish pavlova:* Place pavlova on a flat
serving plate, spread yoghurt over the top
and pour passionfruit over the yoghurt.
Serve within 2 hours but keep in refrigerator until ready to serve.

**Note:** A low cholesterol recipe.

Pawpaw Chiffon Pie
*(see page 100)*

# Pineapple Meringue Pie

*Serves 6.*

**185 g (¾ quantity) rich short crust pastry**
  **(see page 12)**

*Filling:*
**1 medium pineapple**
**3 tablespoons cornflour**
**½ teaspoon salt**
**125 g (½ cup) sugar**
**2 tablespoons cold water**
**juice of ½ lemon**
**2 x 60 g egg yolks**

*Meringue:*
**2 x 60 g egg whites**
**4 tablespoons castor sugar**

Make pastry according to recipe and chill well.

*Filling:* Peel pineapple and cut into 2.5 cm (1 inch) cubes. Place a quarter of the pineapple in a blender and mix at speed 5 for 10 seconds. Repeat until all pineapple is blended. Place pineapple in a heavy-based saucepan. Blend cornflour, salt and sugar smoothly with water and stir into the pineapple. Bring to the boil, stirring continuously, then simmer for 10 minutes. Add lemon juice and egg yolks and stir over heat until thickened without boiling.

*To finish pie:* Roll pastry out thinly and line a deep 20 cm (8 inch) flan tin. Prick base and bake 'blind', then cool on a wire cooling tray. Pour filling into cool pastry case.

*Meringue:* Whisk egg whites at maximum speed until stiff, then whisk in sugar gradually at maximum speed to form a stiff meringue. Pile meringue on top of filling, covering pineapple mixture completely. Swirl top of meringue with a round-bladed knife. Place in a moderately slow oven at 160°C (325°F) for 15-20 minutes or until meringue is golden. Serve warm or cold.

# Pavlova Pie

*Serves 6-8.*

*Meringue:*
**3 x 60 g egg whites**
**185 g (¾ cup) castor sugar**
**½ teaspoon cornflour**
**½ teaspoon vinegar**
**½ teaspoon vanilla essence**

*Topping:*
**300 ml (1 jar/carton) cream**
**1 punnet strawberries**
**3 Chinese gooseberries**
**4 passionfruit**

*Meringue:* Draw an 18 cm (7 inch) circle on rice paper or on oiled greaseproof paper on a baking tray and sprinkle lightly with cornflour until evenly coated. Whisk egg whites in clean polished bowl of Kenwood mixer at maximum speed until stiff. Add castor sugar, a teaspoonful at a time, slowly and continuously, whisking well at maximum speed to dissolve the sugar. Stop whisking and gently fold in the cornflour, vinegar and vanilla essence with a plastic spatula. Spread meringue mixture over the circle and shape into a cake shape. Place in a cool oven at 100-120°C (200-250°F) for 1½-2 hours, until dry and crisp. Open oven door and cool before removing, then peel off paper and cool on a wire cooling tray.

*Filling:* Whip cream and prepare fruit.

*To finish pavlova:* Place pavlova on a flat serving plate and spread whipped cream over the top. Arrange strawberries and slices of Chinese gooseberry attractively on top and drizzle passionfruit over. Serve within 2 hours but keep in the refrigerator until ready to serve.

Banana Passionfruit Cheesecake
*(see page 104)*

# CHIFFON PIES

The chiffon pie is aptly named because it has a texture as light and airy as a piece of chiffon floating in a gentle breeze. The lightness is achieved by folding stiffly whisked egg whites (or chilled evaporated milk) into the filling.

The power of a Kenwood mixer is a great asset when whipping up a chiffon pie for it takes all the hard work out of whisking the egg whites. Chiffon pies are great favourites in hot weather so you will find many tropical ingredients used in the following recipes such as bananas, rum, macadamia nuts, passionfruit and pawpaw, and they all taste delicious.

# Tip

Use the Kenwood blender or food processor for crumbling biscuits for crumb crusts.

# Macadamia Rum Chiffon Pie

*Serves 12.*

**185 g (¾ quantity) rich short crust pastry (see page 12)**

*Filling:*
**60 ml (¼ cup) cold water**
**2 teaspoons gelatine**
**4 x 60 g eggs**
**2 tablespoons sugar**
**125 ml (½ cup) boiling water**
**3 tablespoons rum**
**finely grated rind of 1 lemon**
**pinch of cream of tartar**
**2 tablespoons castor sugar**
**125 g (1 cup) chopped macadamia nuts**
**300 ml (1 jar/carton) thickened cream**
**1 extra tablespoon rum**
**extra macadamia nuts for decoration**

Prepare pastry according to recipe and chill well.

*Filling:* Place ¼ cup cold water in a measuring cup, sprinkle gelatine over and stir until well mixed. Place in a small pan of hot water, over heat (a hot-water bath) and simmer until gelatine has dissolved. Separate eggs, place yolks in bowl of Kenwood mixer, add sugar and whisk until thick and creamy. Pour in boiling water, beating continuously at maximum speed, then pour into a saucepan. Heat over a very low heat, stirring continuously, until mixture thickens, without boiling. Combine gelatine with custard mixture at equal blood heat, stirring quickly. Leave to cool until thick and partially set, then add 3 tablespoons rum and lemon rind.

*To finish pie:* Roll pastry out thinly and line a 23 cm (9 inch) pie plate. Bake 'blind' in a hot oven at 220°C (425°F) for 10 minutes, remove 'blind' filling and bake for a further 10 minutes. Cool on a wire cooling tray. Pour filling into cold pastry case, spread smooth, then refrigerate until set. Whip cream and fold in the extra rum. Pipe cream in rosettes around edge of chiffon pie and decorate with extra macadamia nuts. Serve lightly chilled as a dessert or with coffee.

# Chocolate Rum Pie

*Serves 6.*

185 g (¾ quantity) rich short crust pastry
   or pâte sucrée (see pages 12, 13)

*Filling:*
2 teaspoons gelatine
1 tablespoon cold water
1 tablespoon cornflour
3 tablespoons sugar
250 ml (1 cup) milk
1 x 60 g egg, separated
60 g (2 oz) dark cooking chocolate, melted
1 tablespoon rum
300 ml (1 jar/carton) cream
chocolate curls or grated chocolate for
   decoration

Make pastry according to recipe and chill
well.

*Filling:* Soak gelatine in cold water in a
small bowl then dissolve in a hot-water
bath. Place cornflour and sugar in a saucepan and blend smoothly with a little of the
measured milk. Stir in remaining milk and
bring to the boil, stirring continuously.
Remove from heat and stir in the egg yolk,
melted chocolate and rum. Quickly stir in
the dissolved gelatine, making sure that
both mixtures are at a lukewarm temperature. Cool until on the point of setting.

*To finish pie:* Roll out pastry and line a
23 cm (9 inch) flan tin. Bake 'blind' then
cool on a wire cooling tray. Whisk egg
white at maximum speed with electric
mixer until stiff. Whip cream. Fold egg
white and half cream into chocolate
mixture with a plastic spatula. Pour filling
into pastry case and chill in refrigerator
until firm. Decorate with rosettes of remaining whipped cream and chocolate curls
before serving.

# Banana Chiffon Pie

*Serves 6-8.*

185 g (¾ quantity) rich short crust pastry
   (see page 12)

*Filling:*
1½ teaspoons gelatine
2 tablespoons cold water
¾ cup mashed banana, approx. 2 large
   bananas

1 tablespoon lemon juice
½ teaspoon grated lemon rind
2 egg yolks
3 tablespoons sugar
2 egg whites
4 tablespoons castor sugar
glacé cherries and angelica for decoration

Prepare pastry according to recipe and
chill well.

*Filling:* Sprinkle gelatine onto cold water
and leave to soften. Place bananas in a
blender and mix at speed 3 for 13 seconds
or until mashed, not puréed. Place bananas
in a heavy-based saucepan. Add lemon
juice and rind, egg yolks, sugar and gelatine mixture to bananas and cook slowly
over a low heat, stirring continuously, until
mixture thickens. Do not boil. Remove from
heat and cool over ice until mixture is
partially set.

*To finish pie:* Roll pastry out thinly and line
a 23 cm (9 inch) flan tin. Place on a baking
tray and bake 'blind' in a hot oven at 220°C
(425°F) for 10 minutes. Remove 'blind'
filling and paper, return flan to oven,
reduce temperature to moderately hot at
190°C (375°F) and bake for a further 15
minutes or until pastry is golden. Remove
from oven and cool. Whisk egg whites in a
clean bowl at maximum speed until stiff,
then gradually add castor sugar, whisking
continuously at maximum speed. Fold
meringue gently into banana mixture. Pour
filling into prepared pastry case and chill
in refrigerator until set. Decorate with
cherries and angelica. Serve cold with
whipped cream.

# Passionfruit Chiffon Pie

*Serves 6.*

185 g (¾ quantity) rich short crust pastry
   or pâte sucrée (see pages 12, 13)

*Filling:*
250 ml (1 cup) evaporated milk, chilled
1 packet lemon jelly crystals
250 ml (1 cup) boiling water
pulp of 4-6 passionfruit
300 ml (1 jar/carton) cream
extra passionfruit for decoration

Make pastry as directed in recipe and chill
well.

*Filling:* Chill evaporated milk until icy cold. Dissolve jelly crystals in boiling water, then leave to cool. (Meanwhile shape and bake pie case.) Whip chilled evaporated milk in the Kenwood mixer, with the whisk, at maximum speed until thick. Add cold jelly and stir until combined. Fold passionfruit pulp in with a spatula.

*To finish pie:* Roll pastry out thinly and line a 23 cm (9 inch) flan tin or pie plate. Bake 'blind', then leave to cool on a wire cooling tray. Pour filling into cold pastry case and chill in refrigerator until set. Whip cream and spread on top of chiffon filling. Serve decorated with extra passionfruit pulp drizzled over the cream.

# Pawpaw Chiffon Pie

*Serves 6.*

**185 g (1 quantity) pâte brisée (see page 12)**

**Filling:**
**1½ tablespoons gelatine**
**60 ml (¼ cup) hot water**
**1 cup pawpaw purée (2 cups coarsely chopped paw paw)**
**60 g (¼ cup) sugar**
**3 x 60 g egg yolks, lightly beaten**
**60 ml (¼ cup) lime or lemon juice**
**3 x 60 g egg whites**
**125 g (½ cup) castor sugar**
**crystallized ginger for decoration**

Prepare pastry according to recipe and chill well.

*Filling:* Sprinkle gelatine over hot water and stir to dissolve. Purée pawpaw, 1 cup at a time, in an electric blender or food processor at maximum speed until smooth. Place pawpaw, sugar and egg yolks in the top of a double-boiler and heat over gently boiling water, stirring constantly until sugar dissolves and mixture thickens, about 20 minutes. Add softened gelatine, stirring until dissolved, and stir in lime or lemon juice. Transfer custard to a cold metal bowl or cake tin, stand in a larger dish of ice cubes and place in refrigerator to chill until thick and partially set, checking every 15 minutes.

*To finish pie:* Roll out pastry on a lightly floured board to a round and line a deep 20 cm (8 inch) flan tin. Bake 'blind', then

allow pastry case to cool. Whisk egg whites at maximum speed in Kenwood mixer until stiff, then gradually add castor sugar, whisking continuously at maximum speed. Gently fold meringue into thickened pawpaw custard. Pour into prepared pastry case and pile high, swirling surface with a plastic spatula. Refrigerate pie for at least 3 hours before serving. Serve decorated with crystallized ginger.

# Prune Chiffon Pie

*Serves 6.*

**185 g (¾ quantity) rich short crust pastry (see page 12)**

**Filling:**
**250 g (1 cup) stoned stewed prunes**
**185 ml (¾ cup) prune juice**
**125 g (½ cup) sugar**
**¼ teaspoon salt**
**finely grated rind and juice of 1 lemon**
**1½ tablespoons gelatine**
**3 tablespoons cold water**
**2 x 60 g egg whites**

Make pastry according to recipe and chill well.

*Filling:* Place stewed prunes and juice in a blender or food processor and mix at speed 5 for 20 seconds to a smooth purée. Pour purée into a saucepan, add sugar, salt, lemon rind and juice and bring to the boil, stirring continuously, to dissolve sugar. Remove from heat. Soak gelatine in cold water in a small bowl for 2 minutes, then dissolve in a hot-water bath and cool to lukewarm. Stirring quickly, combine lukewarm gelatine with lukewarm prune mixture, then leave to cool until thick and partially set.

*To finish pie:* Roll pastry out thinly and line a 23 cm (9 inch) flan tin. Place on a baking tray and bake 'blind' in a hot oven at 220°C (425°F) for 10 minutes, remove 'blind' filling and paper, reduce to moderately hot at 190°C (375°F) and bake for a further 15 minutes or until pastry is golden and cooked. Cool on a wire cooling tray. Place egg whites in clean, polished bowl of Kenwood mixer and whisk at maximum speed for 2 minutes or until stiff. Fold egg whites into prune mixture until smoothly combined. Pour filling into pastry case and leave to set. Serve with whipped cream or yoghurt.

# CRUMB CRUST PIES

When you have to make a dessert for the family in hot or humid weather, a crumb crust pie is the answer. Cool and quick to make, particularly when you can crumble the biscuits in a blender or food processor at the flick of a switch. Fill the crumb crust with a light lemon or delicious chocolate filling, oranges and bananas or even a pumpkin ice cream filling and you'll find these pies will be top favourites with your family.

# Chocolate Ice Cream Pie

*Serves 6-8.*

**1 quantity crumb crust (page 17)**

**Filling:**
**250 ml (1 cup) cold milk**
**1 cup chocolate ice cream**
**85 g packet chocolate instant pudding mix (4-6 servings size)**
**whipped cream and chopped nuts to decorate**

Prepare crumb crust according to recipe and press into a 23 cm (9 inch) pie plate. Chill until firm, at least 1 hour.

*Filling:* Blend milk and ice cream in the chilled Kenwood bowl. Add instant pudding mix and beat at minimum speed for about 1 minute.

*To finish pie:* Pour filling immediately into crumb crust and chill in refrigerator until set. Decorate with rosettes of whipped cream and chopped nuts. Children will enjoy this pie.

# Chocolate Mint Pie

*Serves 8.*

**Crumb crust:**
**60 g (2 tablespoons) copha**
**60 g (2 tablespoons) butter**
**150 g (1 cup) cooking chocolate, chopped**
**185 g (2 cups) desiccated coconut**
**30 g (¼ cup) icing sugar**

**Filling:**
**250 ml (1 cup) evaporated milk, well chilled**
**1 tablespoon sugar**
**2 teaspoons lemon juice**
**1 tablespoon boiling water**
**2 teaspoons instant coffee**
**60 g (2 oz) cooking chocolate, melted**
**1 tablespoon gelatine**
**60 ml (¼ cup) hot water**
**few drops peppermint essence**
**whipped cream and chocolate mints or drops for decoration**

*Crumb crust:* Melt copha, butter and chocolate in the top of a double-boiler over gently bubbling water. Remove from heat, add coconut and icing sugar and mix thoroughly. Press mixture into a 23 cm (9 inch) pie plate and chill for at least 1 hour or until firm.

*Filling:* Whip milk in the chilled Kenwood bowl until thick and creamy. Add sugar and lemon juice gradually. Blend boiling water with instant coffee, combine with melted chocolate and allow to cool. Dissolve gelatine in hot water and cool to lukewarm. Add chocolate mixture and gelatine mixture to whipped milk, stirring quickly. Finally, fold in peppermint essence.

*To finish pie:* Carefully pour filling into prepared crumb crust and chill in refrigerator until set. Decorate with rosettes of whipped cream and halved after-dinner mints or drops.

# Christmas Tree Chocolate Pie

*Serves 8-12.*

**Crumb crust:**
**90 g (3 tablespoons) butter or margarine**
**30 g (1 tablespoon) copha**
**60 g (¼ cup) sugar**
**6 cups cornflakes (loosely packed)**

**Filling:**
**3 tablespoons cocoa**
**2 tablespoons cornflour**
**250 g (1 cup) sugar**
**500 ml (2 cups) milk**
**60 g (2 tablespoons) butter or margarine**
**1 teaspoon vanilla essence**
**whipped cream for decoration**

*Crumb crust:* Melt butter and copha in a saucepan over a low heat. Stir in sugar and remove from heat. Crush cornflakes in either a blender or a food processor, then stir into melted mixture. Press and mould the crumb mixture into a 23 cm (9 inch) diameter pie plate and chill in refrigerator until firm.

*Filling:* Blend cocoa, cornflour and sugar to a smooth paste with a little of the measured milk in a mixing bowl. Scald remaining milk in a saucepan, then pour over blended mixture, stirring continuously. Return all mixture to saucepan and bring to the boil, stirring continuously, then simmer for 1 minute. Remove from heat, stir in butter and vanilla.

*To finish pie:* Pour filling into crumb crust. Cover chocolate filling carefully with clear plastic, cool, then chill in refrigerator until set. Whip cream, place in a paper piping bag and trim end off so that you may pipe a thick line of cream. Using a home-made stencil of a Christmas tree as a guide, pipe the outline of the tree on top of the chocolate filling, then fill in the outline with more lines of cream. Chill until ready to serve. Serve with ice cream if liked. Children will love this pie on the Christmas table.

**Note:** A chocolate blancmange may be substituted for the filling.

# Lemon Ice Box Pie

*Serves 8.*

**Crumb crust:**
**225 g packet wholemeal biscuits**
**45 g (¼ cup) brown sugar**
**½ teaspoon ground cinnamon**
**½ teaspoon ground nutmeg**
**¼ teaspoon ground cloves**
**¼ teaspoon ground ginger**
**90 g (3 tablespoons) butter, melted**

**Filling:**
**375 ml can evaporated milk, well chilled**
**2 x 60 g eggs**
**125 g (½ cup) castor sugar**
**finely grated rind and juice of 1 lemon**
**whipped cream and grated nutmeg for decoration**

*Crumb crust:* Crumble biscuits to crumbs in either a blender or a food processor. Add sugar, spices and melted butter and mix until well combined. Press mixture over the bottom and up the sides of a 23 cm (9 inch) pie plate.

*Filling:* Chill evaporated milk in a freezer tray in freezer until it starts to go mushy around the edge. Separate eggs and mix egg yolks with sugar, lemon rind and lemon juice. Whip evaporated milk in the chilled Kenwood bowl until thick, then fold into egg and lemon mixture. Whisk egg whites until stiff, then fold into mixture.

*To finish pie:* Pour filling into crumb crust and refrigerate until set. Serve decorated with whipped cream and sprinkled with freshly grated nutmeg.

# Orange and Banana Flan

*Serves 6.*

*Crumb crust:*
**225 g packet wholemeal biscuits**
**30 g (¼ cup) finely chopped almonds**
**125 g (½ cup) unsalted butter**

*Custard cream:*
**2 tablespoons sugar**
**finely grated rind of 2 oranges**
**300 ml (approx. 1¼ cups) milk**
**2 egg yolks**
**2 tablespoons cornflour**
**2 tablespoons cream**

*Topping:*
**2 large oranges**
**4 bananas**
**juice of 1 large lemon**

*Glaze:*
**2 teaspoons arrowroot**
**2 tablespoons apricot conserve, sieved**

*Crumb crust:* Crumble biscuits a few at a time either in a blender or a food processor. Chop almonds also in a blender or food processor at maximum speed for 10-12 seconds, then toast them on foil under a hot grill. Melt butter and mix biscuit crumbs, nuts and butter altogether. Place mixture in a 23 cm (9 inch) flan tin or ceramic flan dish. Using the back of a metal spoon, press mixture against the sides and over the base of the tin, making sure it is evenly thick. Refrigerate for 1 hour or until firm.

*Custard cream:* Place sugar, orange rind and milk in the top of a double-boiler and heat over boiling water until sugar has dissolved. Blend egg yolks with cornflour and gradually add warmed milk mixture, stirring well. Return mixture to the top of the double-boiler and stir continuously over boiling water until it thickens. Allow custard to cool, then add cream, beating well.

*To finish flan:* Spread custard over base of flan case and chill in refrigerator for 1 hour or until firm.

*Topping:* Working on a plate to collect juice and using a small serrated stainless steel knife, cut skin and all white pith from oranges. Slice oranges and remove any seeds. Peel and slice bananas at an angle and sprinkle with lemon juice. Arrange orange slices in a circle around top of custard. Drain banana and arrange rows of overlapping banana slices between slices of orange. Refrigerate whilst preparing glaze.

*Glaze:* Pour orange juice on plate into a measuring jug and make up to 150 ml (⅔ cup) with cold water. Blend arrowroot to a smooth paste with a little of the orange liquid, then stir in remaining liquid. Melt apricot conserve in a saucepan, add arrowroot mixture and bring to the boil, stirring constantly, then boil for 1-2 minutes or until mixture clears and thickens. Allow to cool. Brush glaze over surface of flan. Chill before serving.

# Pumpkin Ice Cream Pie

*Serves 8.*

**1 quantity crumb crust (see page 17)**

*Filling:*
**1 tablespoon gelatine**
**125 g (⅔ cup) brown sugar**
**1 teaspoon ground cinnamon**
**½ teaspoon ground ginger**
**¼ teaspoon ground cloves**
**½ teaspoon salt**
**175 ml (approx. ¾ cup) water**
**1 cup puréed cooked pumpkin**
**500 ml (2 cups) vanilla ice cream**
**3 tablespoons thinly sliced almonds**

Prepare crumb crust according to recipe and press over the base and up the sides of a 23 cm (9 inch) round pie plate. Bake in a moderate oven at 180°C (350°F) for 6 minutes. Cool.

*Filling:* Place gelatine, brown sugar, spices and salt in a saucepan. Stir in water with a wooden spoon and bring to the boil over a medium heat, stirring constantly. Remove from heat. Mix pumpkin to a purée in either a blender or a food processor. Stir pumpkin and ice cream into spice mixture and chill until mixture is at setting point.

*To finish pie:* Pour filling into crumb crust and chill overnight or until set. Spread sliced almonds over a baking tray and place in a moderate oven at 180°C (350°F) for 5 minutes or until golden. Cool. Sprinkle golden almonds on top of pumpkin pie. Serve pie for dessert.

# CHEESECAKES

The rich baked cheesecakes and the lighter textured gelatine cheesecakes are ever-popular pies for a party dessert. The richer baked cheesecakes are European in origin and are good winter desserts. They also freeze well. The gelatine cheesecakes are set in the refrigerator and are best served slightly chilled, so they are ideal summer desserts. These do not freeze well. Most of the cheesecake recipes which follow are made in a delicious crumb crust.

# Tip

Make sure cream and cottage cheeses are at room temperature as they cream quicker and are smoother than when used straight from the refrigerator.

# Banana Passionfruit Cheesecake

*Serves 8-12.*

**1 quantity crumb crust (see page 17)**
**¼ teaspoon each ground cinnamon and ground nutmeg**

*Filling:*
**1 tablespoon gelatine**
**3 tablespoons cold water**
**1 tablespoon finely grated lemon rind**
**250 g (1 cup) cottage cheese**
**250 g (1 cup) castor sugar**
**3 tablespoons lemon juice**
**375 ml can evaporated milk, well chilled**
**3 bananas, sliced**
**2 passionfruit**

*Topping:*
**2 tablespoons sugar**
**1 tablespoon arrowroot or cornflour**
**125 ml (½ cup) lemon juice**
**3 passionfruit**

Prepare crumb crust according to recipe and add ¼ teaspoon each ground cinnamon and nutmeg to the biscuit crumbs. Press mixture over the bottom and up side of a 20 cm (8 inch) spring-form tin and chill in refrigerator.

*Filling:* Soften gelatine in cold water, add lemon rind and heat in a hot-water bath until gelatine is dissolved. Cool to lukewarm. Sieve cottage cheese into Kenwood bowl, add sugar and beat well. Add gelatine, beating continuously, then add lemon juice and mix well. Chill until partially set. Whip evaporated milk in the chilled Kenwood bowl until stiff. Fold into cottage cheese mixture.

*To finish cheesecake:* Pour half filling into the crumb crust, cover with sliced bananas and passionfruit, then pour remaining filling over. Chill in refrigerator until set, 6-8 hours, overnight if possible.

*Topping:* Blend sugar and arrowroot with lemon juice and passionfruit pulp in a small saucepan. Bring to the boil, stirring continuously. Add a few drops edible yellow food colouring if liked. Cool topping, then carefully remove cheesecake from tin and spread topping over the top. Refrigerate until ready to serve.

# Boysenberry Cheesecake

*Serves 8-12.*

**Crumb crust:**
**225 g packet ginger biscuits**
**125 g (½ cup) butter, melted**

**Filling:**
**500 g (2 cups) packaged cream cheese**
**300 ml (1 jar/carton) sour cream**
**2 x 60 g eggs, separated**
**1 tablespoon gelatine**
**3 tablespoons cold water**
**125 g (½ cup) castor sugar**
**425 g can boysenberries, drained**

*Crumb crust:* Crush ginger biscuits into fine crumbs in a blender or food processor. Add melted butter and mix well. Press the crumb mixture over the bottom and sides of a 20 cm (8 inch) spring-form tin. Chill in refrigerator until firm.

*Filing:* Sieve cream cheese into the Kenwood bowl. Add sour cream and mix well. Add egg yolks and beat well. Dissolve gelatine in 3 tablespoons cold water in a hot-water bath. Cool to lukewarm, then quickly mix into cheese filling. Stir in the sugar. Whisk egg whites in the electric mixer until stiff. Fold egg whites into cream cheese mixture along with the boysenberries, but reserve a few firm ones for decoration.

*To finish cheesecake:* Pour mixture into the biscuit crust and chill in refrigerator until set, overnight if possible. Turn cheesecake out onto a serving plate and decorate with reserved berries.

# Christmas Cottage Cheese Pie

*Serves 8.*

**250 g (1 quantity) short crust pastry (see page 11)**

**Filling:**
**250 g (1 cup) cottage cheese**
**2 x 60 g eggs**
**60 g (¼ cup) castor sugar**
**1 teaspoon vanilla essence**
**1 cup fruit mince**

Make pastry according to recipe and line a 23 cm (9 inch) pie plate. Bake 'blind' in a hot oven at 200°C (400°F) for 10 minutes. Remove 'blind' filling and paper and allow to cool.

*Filling:* Beat cottage cheese, eggs, sugar and vanilla in an electric mixer at medium speed for 1 minute, increase speed to maximum for a further 30 seconds.

*To finish pie:* Spread fruit mince over base of pastry case. Spoon cottage cheese mixture on top and spread smooth. Bake in a moderately hot oven at 190°C (375°F) for 25 minutes. Allow to cool slowly, then chill before serving. Serve topped with a sprig of holly.

# Grapefruit Cheesecake

*Serves 8-12.*

**1 quantity crumb crust (see page 17)**
**1 teaspoon each ground cinnamon and nutmeg and ¼ teaspoon ground cloves**

**Filling:**
**2 grapefruit**
**2 x 60 g eggs**
**185 g (¾ cup) sugar**
**1 tablespoon gelatine**
**375 g (1½ cups) packaged cream cheese**
**finely grated rind and juice of 1 lemon**
**300 ml (1 jar/carton) cream**
**extra 200 ml (1 small jar) cream and 1 passionfruit for decoration**

Prepare crumb crust according to recipe and add 1 teaspoon each ground cinnamon and nutmeg and ¼ teaspoon ground cloves to biscuit crumbs. Press mixture over the bottom and mould up the sides of a 20 cm (8 inch) spring-form tin. Chill in refrigerator until firm.

*Filling:* Peel grapefruit using a small serrated knife, working on a plate to catch the juice. Cut all white pith off carefully and cut grapefruit into segments, cutting closely on either side of the membranes. Reserve 8 grapefruit segments for decoration and chop the remainder. Reserve ½ cup grapefruit juice. Separate 1 egg and place egg yolk in the top of a double-boiler. Add remaining egg and sugar and beat over gently bubbling water until thick and creamy. Cool to lukewarm. Dissolve gelatine in 3 tablespoons of the measured grapefruit juice, cool to lukewarm and stir quickly into the egg mixture. Sieve cream cheese into the Kenwood bowl, add chopped grapefruit, remaining grapefruit juice, lemon rind and juice and egg mixture and mix together just until evenly combined. Whisk egg white until stiff. Whip cream until thick and fluffy. Fold both whisked egg white and whipped cream into cheese mixture.

*To finish cheesecake:* Pour filling into crumb crust and place in refrigerator until set. Remove cheesecake carefully from tin and decorate with whipped cream, reserved grapefruit segments and passion-fruit pulp before serving.

# Pineapple and Ginger Cheesecake

*Serves 8-12.*
**1 quantity crumb crust (see page 17)**
**1 teaspoon ground ginger**

*Filling:*
**1½ tablespoons gelatine**
**125 ml (½ cup) pineapple juice**
**500 g (2 cups) cottage cheese, sieved**
**250 g (1 cup) castor sugar**
**finely grated rind of 1 lemon**
**3 tablespoons lemon juice**
**1 cup drained, finely chopped fresh pineapple**
**½ cup chopped preserved ginger in syrup**
**250 ml (1 cup) sour cream**
**200 ml (1 small jar) cream and extra preserved ginger for decoration**

Prepare crumb crust according to recipe, adding ground ginger to biscuit crumbs. Press mixture over the base and up sides of a greased 20 cm (8 inch) spring-form tin. Chill well in refrigerator until firm.

*Filling:* Soften gelatine in pineapple juice for 2-3 minutes, then dissolve in a hot-water bath (by standing container in a larger container of boiling water). Beat cottage cheese, sugar, lemon rind and juice together in the Kenwood bowl until well combined. Stir lukewarm gelatine mixture into cottage cheese mixture, then chill in refrigerator for 30 minutes. Beat cottage cheese mixture to a smooth texture, then stir in pineapple, chopped preserved ginger and sour cream until evenly combined.

*To finish cheesecake:* Pour filling into the

Crumb crust, cover and chill in refrigerator for 2-3 hours or overnight until filling is firm. Whip cream until thick and pipe large swirls around edge of cheesecake. Cut preserved ginger into short slivers and sprinkle on top of cream. Serve cheesecake slightly chilled.

# Strawberry Cheesecake

*Serves 8-12.*

**1 quantity crumb crust (see page 17)**
**½ teaspoon each ground cinnamon, cloves and nutmeg**

*Filling:*
**250 g (1 cup) packaged cream cheese**
**250 g (1 cup) cottage cheese**
**3 x 60 g eggs**
**2 tablespoons cornflour**
**250 g (1 cup) castor sugar**
**250 ml (1 cup) sour cream**
**finely grated rind of 1 lemon**
**3 tablespoons lemon juice**

*Topping:*
**1 punnet large strawberries**
**6 tablespoons redcurrant jelly**

Prepare crumb crust according to recipe, adding ground cinnamon, cloves and nutmeg to the crumbs. Press mixture over the base and up side of a 20 cm (8 inch) buttered spring-form tin. Place in refrigerator for 1 hour.

*Filling:* Sieve cheeses then mix together in electric mixer or food processor until smooth. Add eggs, one at a time, and beat well until smooth. Add cornflour and sugar and mix well. Finally, add sour cream, lemon rind and juice and mix well.

*To finish cheesecake:* Pour mixture into prepared crumb crust and bake in the middle of a moderately slow oven at 170°C (325°F) for 1½ hours. Open oven door and leave cheesecake in cooling oven to cool. Chill in refrigerator for a few hours or overnight. Loosen crumb crust carefully from edge of tin with a round-bladed knife, then remove side and base of spring-form tin.

*Topping:* Slice strawberries and place in a layer on top of cheesecake. Melt redcurrant jelly in saucepan and brush glaze over strawberries. Chill slightly to set glaze before serving.

# Sultana and Almond Cheesecake

*Serves 8.*

**1 quantity crumb crust (see page 17)**

*Filling:*
**375 g (1½ cups) packaged cream cheese**
**125 ml (½ cup) sour cream**
**3 x 60 g eggs**
**185 g (¾ cup) castor sugar**
**2 tablespoons cornflour**
**finely grated rind of 1 lemon**
**1 tablespoon lemon juice**
**3 tablespoons sultanas**
**2 tablespoons slivered almonds**

Prepare crumb crust according to recipe and press into a lightly greased 20 cm (8 inch) spring-form tin and refrigerate until firm.

*Filling:* Place cream cheese into the Kenwood bowl and beat at maximum speed until smooth and creamy, add sour cream and beat 1 minute longer. Add eggs, one at a time, beating well after each addition. Mix in sugar, cornflour, lemon rind and juice at maximum speed. Reduce to speed 1 and add sultanas.

*To finish cheesecake:* Pour filling into prepared crumb crust and sprinkle surface with slivered almonds. Stand tin on a baking tray and bake in the centre of a moderately slow oven at 160°C (325°F) for 45-50 minutes. Allow to cool in oven. Refrigerate for several hours before serving.

# Yoghurt Pie

*Serves 8.*

*Crumb crust:*
**225 g packet wholemeal biscuits**
**90 g (3 tablespoons) polyunsaturated margarine**
**2 tablespoons honey**

*Filling:*
**250 g ( 1cup) packaged cream cheese**
**250 ml (1 cup) thick yoghurt**
**2 x 60 g eggs**
**1½ tablespoons honey**
**90 g (½ cup) raisins**
**½ cup canned or stewed apricots, finely chopped**

*Crumb crust:* Break biscuits in half and place in a blender, about a third at a time, mix at maximum speed for 20 seconds or until biscuits are crushed. Pour biscuit crumbs into a mixing bowl. Repeat until all biscuits are crushed. Melt margarine and honey in a saucepan over a low heat, add to biscuit crumbs and mix thoroughly. Cool slightly, then press into a 20 cm (8 inch) pie plate or flan ring and refrigerate until firm and set.

*Filling:* Whisk cheese in Kenwood bowl on speed 5 for about 30 seconds until fluffy, then gradually add yoghurt, eggs and honey and continue to whisk for another 30 seconds until smooth. Stir in fruit.

*To finish pie:* Pour filling into the crumb crust and bake in a moderately hot oven at 190°C (375°F) for 25-30 minutes or until set. Chill well before serving.

# INDEX